Ryan,

Live

Love

Thrive!;

NO TURNING BACK

NO TURNING BACK

One Man's Inspiring True Story of
Courage, Determination, and Hope

BRYAN ANDERSON
with
DAVID ALAN MACK

BERKLEY BOOKS, NEW YORK

THE BERKLEY PUBLISHING GROUP
Published by the Penguin Group
Penguin Group (USA) Inc.
375 Hudson Street, New York, New York 10014, USA
Penguin Group (Canada), 90 Englinton Avenue East, Suite 700, Toronto, Ontario M4P 2Y3 Canada
(a division of Pearson Penguin Canada Inc.)
Penguin Books Ltd., 80 Strand, London WC2R 0RL, England
Penguin Group Ireland, 25 St. Stephen's Green, Dublin 2, Ireland (a division of Penguin Books Ltd.)
Penguin Group (Australia), 250 Camberwell Road, Camberwell, Victoria 3124, Australia
(a division of Pearson Australia Group Pty. Ltd.)
Penguin Books India Pvt. Ltd., 11 Community Centre, Panchsheel Park, New Delhi—110 017, India
Penguin Group (NZ), 67 Apollo Drive, Rosedale, Auckland, 0632, New Zealand
(a division of Pearson New Zealand Ltd.)
Penguin Books (South Africa) (Pty.) Ltd., 24 Sturdee Avenue, Rosebank, Johannesburg 2196,
South Africa

Penguin Books Ltd., Registered Offices: 80 Strand, London, WC2R, 0RL England

This book is an original publication of The Berkley Publishing Group.

The publisher does not have any control over and does not assume any responsibility for author or third-party websites or their content.

NO TURNING BACK

"Survive" lyrics and music written by Rise Against: Timothy McIlrath, Christopher Chasse, Joseph Daniel Principe, and Brandon Barnes. © 2006 Rise Against. All rights reserved. Used by permission of Sony ATV Music Publishing.

Copyright © 2011 by Bryan Anderson
Book design by Laura K. Corless

First edition: November 2011

ISBN: 978-0-425-24355-8

PRINTED IN THE UNITED STATES OF AMERICA

10 9 8 7 6 5 4 3 2 1

Penguin is committed to publishing works of quality and integrity.
In that spirit, we are proud to offer this book to our readers;
however, the story, the experiences, and the words
are the author's alone.

To my family and friends, who were, and are always there for me. Especially my mom, who spent thirteen months by my side at Walter Reed. To the people of Chicago who warmly welcomed me at my homecoming and accepted me as I am and continue to support me. To the soldiers returning from Iraq and Afghanistan, in the hope that they may find some little bit of wisdom in these pages that may help them in some small way.

Life for you has been less than kind
So take a number, stand in line
We've all been sorry, we've all been hurt
But how we survive is what makes us who we are

—Rise Against, *The Sufferer & the Witness*, "Survive"

CONTENTS

CONTENTS

FOREWORD

By Gary Sinise

I first met Bryan Anderson in 2006, not too long after he arrived at Walter Reed Army Medical Center. I have been visiting the hospital regularly since 2003, and over the years have met many severely wounded warriors. Bryan was the second triple amputee I had met there and when I walked into the physical therapy room there he was, up on his legs and smiling, eager to tell me his story and with the most amazing and upbeat attitude.

It turned out that we are both originally from Illinois and we shared stories of familiar places where we had grown up. His spirit was infectious and I was immediately drawn to him. In the picture included here, you can see that smile—a smile that immediately put everyone he came in contact with at ease.

Bryan knew that for most visitors to the hospital, coming

in contact with someone who was missing both his legs and an arm might be difficult, so he went out of his way to joke and laugh and go on as if nothing was different. He had begun to accept what had happened to him and was looking toward the future—a future of what he could do, not what he couldn't do.

That positive attitude of living each moment of one's life for everything it's worth is at the core of who Bryan Anderson is.

After that first meeting, I would see Bryan from time to time back at the hospital or at other events around the country—like the Friday night dinners for wounded warriors at Fran O'Brien's restaurant, hosted by Vietnam veteran Hal Koster, or back in Illinois at the USO gala or at a concert I was playing with my band, the Lt. Dan Band. Whenever I can, I try to let Bryan know where I am going to be and am always thrilled to see him at an event or concert.

And then, in January 2007, there he is on the cover of *Esquire* magazine! Clearly his story caught the attention of the national media, and for good reason. It is a harrowing and inspiring story and Bryan is an exceptional individual. The *Esquire* story also caught the attention of my fellow producers on *CSI: NY* and they asked if I knew him. Boom! Bryan was featured as a murder suspect in one of our episodes. He's a natural.

In April 2009, on another visit to Walter Reed, I met Brendan Marrocco, the first soldier to survive losing all four limbs in a bombing in Iraq. As I drove away from the hospital, I called Bryan and told him about Brendan. I thought perhaps he could help and asked if there was any way that he could visit him.

Within days, Bryan was at Brendan's bedside and I know that for Brendan, having Bryan there at that critical stage was extremely helpful. To Bryan, this was a no-brainer. Of course he would go, as he has taken what has happened to him and turned it into motivation for others.

Whenever I see Bryan, he renews my faith that anything, no matter how tough it is, can be overcome. It is because of men and women like Bryan, those who have given so much in service to our country, that I am constantly energized to keep up the important work on behalf of our service members through the Gary Sinise Foundation.

Bryan Anderson is just simply a great American who inspires me and I am proud to call him my friend. It is an honor to know him and I am thrilled that he has decided to share his story in this wonderful book so that more of our fellow citizens will have the chance to know him as well.

God Bless.

Gary Sinise
July 27, 2011

AUTHOR'S NOTE

Hi, I'm Bryan Anderson. Before you dig into this book, there are a few things I think you should know. First, I was a soldier, and I still talk like one—in other words, I swear. So if bad words bother you, just squint and pretend you don't see them.

Second, I know that some people see a book by a triple-amputee veteran and make a lot of assumptions. I want you to know this book is not about the war in Iraq, and I'm not pushing a political agenda. This book is about my experiences and what I've learned from them.

Third, I know what I believe about God, but this book's not about that either. I'm not trying to sell you on religion or talk you out of it. I've got no ax to grind there.

Fourth, even though I'm going to tell you about the day I was wounded and what I went through during rehab at Walter Reed, this book is not just some war memoir or a pity party. I'm not looking for praise or sympathy. I just want to share some of my stories with you.

This book is not about being wounded. It's not about struggling. This book is about living.

It's about life.

NO TURNING BACK

1

ALIVE DAY

On the day I got blown up, it was hot as hell. It was about eleven o'clock in the morning on October 23, 2005, in sunny downtown Baghdad, Iraq, and if I had to guess, I'd say it was a hundred and thirty degrees in the shade.

I was a specialist in the U.S. Army, 411th Military Police Company. Me and my guys were on our second tour in Iraq. We'd been designated as the "commander's escort." We were like a personal security detail for our commanding officer, who we'd nicknamed "Captain America" because whatever happened anywhere in Baghdad, he just wanted to be in the thick of it. Whenever anything happened, he was like "Let's go! I want to do this! I want to get involved! I wanna conquer the world!"

Before you get the wrong idea, let me just say that I think his attitude was not a good thing. In my opinion, he was putting our lives in danger for no reason, just because he wanted people to think he was a "hands-on" kind of leader.

The reason we'd gotten stuck on that crap detail was that we'd worked with him once, and he'd said, "You know what? These are the people that I want to come out with me. They know their shit, they know what they're doing." Our punishment for being competent was getting to babysit him everywhere he went for the next year. Lucky us.

It's not like he didn't have plenty of other people to choose from. A company is roughly 150 soldiers, divided into four platoons, all doing a variety of missions. As MPs (military police officers), we had several tasks: We were training Iraqi police officers at the police academy. We were also going out to the police stations and teaching them basic upkeep; we taught them to maintain clean jail cells and how to stock enough food, ammunition, weapons, vehicles, and other supplies. We made sure they knew how to do a patrol and how to do a raid.

Other MPs handled transport security, such as MSR patrol, which is guarding a main supply route. In other words, if there was a main road that our troops traveled on a lot, we'd drive up and down it, making sure people weren't laying IEDs (improvised explosive devices) and stuff like that. Some folks manned the gate and guarded the base. Everybody had a job to do.

For me and seven of my buddies, our job was driving Captain America through downtown hell.

Every day we would go and visit the Iraqi police stations. If any of our guys got hit by an IED, or if there was an attack, we would divert and respond to that, but the bulk of our work was a daily tour of the Iraqi police stations. We didn't understand why we were going there; there were squad leaders and platoon sergeants who were designated to supervise those operations. If the CO had wanted to go out there once a week just to make sure nothing had burned down, that would've been okay, but every day? The noncoms manning those stations knew their jobs, and they were doing them just fine. I can't tell you how many times I wanted to say to Captain America, "There's simply no reason to go out there every day. You're not the one that's doing the job. And by going out there every day, you're pissing off your sergeants by making them feel like you don't trust them. Plus, you're putting nine lives in danger that you don't really need to."

That's how I felt, but I didn't get a say in the matter, so that morning me and my guys saddled up for another tour of Baghdad's police stations. Every morning, we would get up about an hour before we had to leave. That morning we got up around ten because we'd been on a mission late the night before. My team and I were wearing DCUs (desert camouflage uniforms) with long sleeves, and we had our Kevlar helmets and twenty-five-pound body-armor vests with shoulder pads and kidney pads. I was wearing my nine-millimeter pistol in my right thigh holster. I also had a sawed-off twelve-gauge pump-action shotgun (for entry through locked doors; you'd blow the lock—*BOOM!*—and then kick the door open) and a SAW (squad automatic weapon) M249, a fully automatic belt-fed machine gun. Because I was the driver, I got the M249, and since I was also an entry man, I got the shotgun, too. Being an MP, I carried my nine-mil—not everyone gets nine-mils. Not everybody gets a lot of things, but because of my multiple jobs I was all weaponed up.

As the driver, I had to make sure my truck was good to go. It's called a PMCS, which stands for "preventive maintenance checks and services." I checked the oil, the tires and the air filter, and then I made sure there was gas in it. Of course, after every mission you always top off—always. You never know when you might get sent out again, so you've always gotta be ready. Next, I started putting my gear where I needed it to go. The gunner, Brad Gietzel, started mounting the gun on top of the truck. Me and my pal Kenny Olson were sitting up front, setting the radios, making sure that they worked and that we had communication with the TOCC (Tactical Operations Command Center).

At around eleven o'clock, we headed out.

Inside the truck, it was really hot. Most of the trucks had air-conditioning, but in half of them it didn't work. When it did, it wasn't strong, and it didn't cool the truck down. My truck—and once you're assigned a truck, it's your truck—had working a/c, but to be honest, it didn't do shit. At the end of the day, when I'd get off mission and take off my body armor, my DCUs would look like I'd just jumped in a pool. I mean, they'd be drenched. From the moment I stepped outside in Iraq, I was sweating my balls off. The only time I was comfortable was when I was back at base and in PTs—a T-shirt and shorts. That's it. When I didn't have body armor on and could just walk around the base in DCUs, it wasn't so bad either. But being on a mission, all suited up in the heat, it sucked.

My Humvee's interior was a cramped, green oven. It stank of diesel fumes from the engine. The housing for the drivetrain ran up the middle of the cab, and it got really hot. If my leg was up against it, it'd cook to medium rare in about a minute. And there was always dust from the street everywhere—up my nose, in my throat, coating my teeth with grit.

The other thing I noticed inside the truck was the hum. When the engine was running, I felt it—not just with my hands on the steering wheel but in the seat of my pants. Near the end of my first year and the start of my second year in Iraq, that hum and the feeling that went with it kind of made me feel comfortable—safe. I could fall asleep inside or on top of my truck, no problem. I came to think of my truck as a safe place—maybe the only safe place I had.

You see, I thought the protection on my Humvee was pretty good. It was an up-armored model already, with added steel plating and ballistic-resistant windows, and then my squad and I had put some soft armor—aluminum plates—on the truck ourselves. We put plates on the turret guard, the gunner's shield, and the extra plates that go on the doors. So we thought we had a pretty good ride. Whenever I did my services-and-maintenances, I was sure I had a pretty kick-ass truck.

But it wasn't just about the armor. My truck was like my home. When I was in the driver's seat, I had everything I needed. On my right, I always had a Pepsi and a bag of sunflower seeds. Kenny, who rode shotgun, always drank Dr Pepper. There was a lot of space between all of us inside the vehicle. The radio mount separated me and Kenny, and Gietzel was well behind us in the middle of the truck. Behind Gietzel, at the back of the truck, we had a cooler in the middle on the floor, and it was stocked with water and Gatorade.

My M249 and my shotgun were lying on the floor to the right of my seat.

Slung from the top in the back, tucked into the back corner of the overhead, we had our M136 AT4 cannon—an antitank weapon.

5

We'd set it up so that all Gietzel needed to do was pull a string. That would undo a slipknot and drop the weapon right into his hands, so he could just pick it up and open fire, if he'd needed to.

Over my head, by the visor, I'd made a mesh web out of 550 cord, which looks like green rope but is actually a multipurpose nylon cord. If you cut 550 cord, inside it has a bunch of smaller white fibers braided together, and you can pull out individual strands if you need to do something small. I'd tied some of those white strands into a net so I could store stuff above my visor. I had a little notebook with nine-line medevac instructions. For a medevac, there are nine things you have to say when you're calling in a helicopter to come pick up a wounded soldier—*What's the injury? How bad is it? Where are you? Is it coalition forces or Iraqi forces?* and so on—so it's nice to just have that book right there and be able to follow the steps and not have to think about it.

I also kept a pack of gum up in the net, and my gloves always went up there. So did my goggles, glasses, sunglasses, or whatever. I also stowed my iPod up there, in the corner, along with a pair of sports earphones. Those always stayed in the truck. I'd made it so I could just pull one earphone down and put it on my left ear so I could hear everything that was going on to my right inside the truck—my buddies, the radio, and all that—and still, at the same time, rock out to my music. I also had speakers up there, for times when all of us felt like hearing some tunes, such as when we were hanging out in the motor pool or elsewhere on base. The best part? As the driver (and owner of the iPod), I got to pick the music. We'd listen to rock, punk, and even some soft stuff. One of our favorites was Linkin Park.

Technically, I wasn't supposed to have the iPod in the truck, but whether it came out or not depended on who was in my truck. If it was just me and my guys, it was no big deal, but the iPod stayed out of sight when the commander or some other big shot rode with us.

Most of all though, when I was in my truck I felt I had more control over my destiny. In the barracks you had mortar rounds coming at you and you never knew where they were gonna hit. All you could do was run for cover. But in my truck I had my weapons, I was mobile, and I could take action. I could find out where the danger was coming from and take care of it.

But I didn't have much control the day I got blown up.

The day was just getting started. We were only a mile or two from base.

My first year in Iraq, I'd just plowed through traffic. If any cars got in my way, I'd push them clear with my truck. I'd smashed a bunch of cars—it had been kind of fun.

During my second tour, the Army changed the protocol because of all the vehicle IEDs. We started calling them VBIDs (vehicle-borne improvised explosive devices). To deal with that new threat, we'd started leaving a cushion. We would get behind traffic and stay back 250 yards so that there was a nice bubble between us and the civilian vehicles. Then we wouldn't let anyone get within 250 yards behind us either.

So we had five football fields' worth of empty road, and we were driving.

To make this protocol work, you can't drive very fast. You end up cruising at around five miles per hour. Bored, I was slouched in my seat, with my hands together at the bottom of the steering

7

wheel. I sat with my left leg curled up under my right leg, which was down for driving—half Indian style. Kenny and I were passing the time bullshitting, and he said something funny about our CO. I laughed as I took my right hand off the steering wheel and reached down to grab my smokes. Now, I wasn't supposed to smoke in my Humvee. It's against regs, but I didn't give a shit since Captain America was in the lead truck and I was in the rear truck. So I grabbed my smokes and pulled one out, and I was still lookin' at Kenny because we were still talking.

As I lit my cigarette, the explosion went off.

For some reason, I didn't hear it. I only saw it, out of the corner of my eye, to the left of me. The next thing I knew, everything was completely pitch-black. I couldn't see anything. It wasn't because I was knocked out. There was just so much smoke inside the truck that I couldn't see shit. My first reaction was to look to my right, where everyone else was in relation to me inside the truck, and I called out, "Hey! Are you all right? We just got hit!"

I didn't hear anything—nobody answered. And I thought, *Shit! Are they dead?* Twisting around, I strained to see through the smoke.

Understand that I had no idea I'd been hit; at that point I was worried only about my guys, not myself. I didn't feel anything, no pain—not yet, anyway. So I struggled to pierce the curtain of smoke, but I saw nothing but green. I was totally confused. *Why am I seeing green?* I tried to sit back in my seat, but when I did, I rolled onto my back, and my head fell backward. Then I wondered, *Why did my head fall backward?*

When the explosion went off, it had cut off my legs and left hand instantly. My legs were on the floorboard, my hand was in the passenger seat—Kenny told me later that my hand had hit him in the face—and the blast had spun me sideways, so that I was lying on my back in my seat. When I'd looked to my right and saw green, I'd been looking at the back of my seat.

After my head fell backward, I figured out I was on my back. While I was lying there, I couldn't see anything, but I was trying to figure out where everybody was and if anybody in my truck was dead, because I didn't know. Then, for some reason, I thought, *All right, get out! Get out of the truck!* But I couldn't. I had no idea why I couldn't get out, but I simply couldn't make it happen. So I started shouting, "Yo! I can't get out! Help! Help!"

The reason no one had answered when I'd called out earlier was that Kenny and Gietzel had jumped out immediately. Kenny, it turned out, had some shrapnel in his hip and his wrist, as well as number of superficial wounds, and Gietzel had caught some shrapnel in his ass—the *Forrest Gump* wound. When he'd jumped out, he'd landed on his back and started croaking, "Ow! My ass, my ass!" He stayed down as Kenny ran to the truck in front of us, the second truck.

The driver of the second truck was Michael Wait. Wait opened his door, and he and Kenny both looked back at my truck. Wait said, "Hey, Anderson's not out of the vehicle yet! Let's go back and get him!" They ran back. I think Kenny had an idea what they were gonna find, because he had seen my severed hand on the passenger seat when he'd gotten out.

I was lying in the truck, bleeding and unable to move, when I heard them start to work on my door. In Iraq, we combat-locked the doors. There were two steel plates that slid down over the frame so that nobody could just yank open the doors. We needed that because the doors on military vehicles don't have regular locks. What the insurgents had started doing was running up, opening the doors, and yanking soldiers out of the Humvees. To prevent that, we'd started combat-locking our trucks. It also helped against IEDs, because when the big ones started going off, they had been blowing our doors open. That had been a big part of what was getting our guys killed: once the doors were open, all the after-shit poured in—fire, smoke, and shrapnel. So this extra precaution had become part of our protocol.

Well, in my situation, that kind of sucked because I was in no shape to operate my lock like the other guys had been able to do.

Luckily, we had just gotten some special tools that looked like small tire irons and were made to fit the bolts on the outside of the door. Those locks would just fall off once you turned those bolts. Thanks to those tools, Wait and Kenny got me out of the vehicle in under thirty seconds. I mean, it was really fast. Kenny and Wait each undid a bolt and spun 'em loose, and then Wait opened the door. He saw me, and he just kind of froze. He just stood there with his mouth half open, staring at me, not making a sound. Kenny put his hand on Wait's back and pushed him forward as he said, "Just go! Just go! We'll think about it later!"

Wait pulled me out of the truck. As I cleared the door frame, I got a breath of fresh air—well, as fresh as you're gonna get when it's 120 degrees in southeast Baghdad and you're next to a smoldering truck, but it was better than what I'd been breathing inside the Humvee—and it sharpened me right up. I was still in shock, but I was completely aware of what was going on.

Kenny and Wait got me to the sidewalk and laid me down. As I lay on the dusty pavement, I was thinking, "All right, what's going on? Are we being shot at? Do I need to be shooting somebody right now? What's happening? Are we being attacked?" But mostly I was thinking, "Shit! My mom's gonna kill me!"

I was looking around and trying to get a handle on where everyone was and what they were doing. I knew I was in shock, and my eyes were just wandering. I think I was just searching for something to lock onto—gunfire or some other sign we were being attacked, something that would let me know what I needed to do next. I was really just kind of concentrating and asking myself, *Do I hear gunfire? Do I hear explosions? Do I hear anything?*

All I could see was my friends running back and forth between me and the second truck, over and over, so I figured out we weren't still being attacked. *Okay,* I thought, *we're clear.*

At that point I was able to kind of relax, but as I kept looking at my friends, I knew something was wrong. I knew I'd had to be pulled out of the vehicle, that I hadn't been able to get out by myself, so I knew that there had to be something wrong. I just didn't know what yet.

I sensed there was blood all over my face.

The flies in Iraq are really nasty, and they were buzzing around my eyes like something out of *The Exorcist,* and I raised my right hand to swat them away.

That's when I noticed for the first time that the tip of my index finger was gone.

Well, *that* got my attention. My whole hand looked like ground beef stuck together with dirt, but I knew my friends couldn't be freaking out about that. Then I turned my hand over to see the back of it, and I saw there was a whole chunk of it missing between my thumb and forefinger. I could see into my hand, right down to

11

the shattered bones and the torn ligaments and shredded muscles. It was really nasty.

But as I looked at my hand, I was thinking, *Well, that's not so bad.*

I was still trying to figure out why my friends were freaking out when a fat-ass horsefly landed on my eye. I lifted my left hand to shoo it away, and there was nothing—I just whiffed. That was a "whoa" moment. I looked over, and my left sleeve was just kind of hanging. It was soaked and dripping with blood.

As I stared at that empty space where my left hand used to be, all I could think was, *Fuck.*

That, I figured, could maybe be what my guys were losing their shit over. So I looked back at them, and then I looked up at my arm, and I thought to myself, *Okay, but that's not that bad. That's not gonna kill me.* That's what I told myself while I was lying there.

Then I looked down.

As I tried to lift my head off the asphalt to look at the rest of my body, Wait tried to force my head back onto the ground, to stop me from seeing what had happened, but it was too late; I'd already seen what had happened.

My legs were gone.

The first thought that went through my head was, *Fuck—that did not just happen.*

But it had. After I took a few seconds to process it, I decided, *Well, things are gonna be a little different from now on.*

I looked up, and for the first time since being pulled from the Humvee, I made direct eye contact with someone. I knew I needed to say something to my guys, but I didn't know what to tell them. I don't know why, but I reached up and grabbed Wait's arm and said, "Holy shit, dude! Do you think I'll ever get laid again?" And he started laughing.

Later on, he told me, "When you said that, it made me realize that you were still in there. It wasn't just a body on a sidewalk." That put him back on track. Before I'd said that, he'd been fumbling with the tourniquets and all that stuff, but once I'd cracked a joke, he just snapped into action, and it was all like *boom-boom-boom*. The doctors said they'd never seen even medics put on tourniquets as well as Wait had that day. They were beyond good—they were perfect.

Once all the tourniquets were tied, Wait and Kenny sat with me while I lay there for twelve minutes, waiting for the medevac chopper.

With time to think, I finally noticed the pain. My body was in shock, so most of what I felt was a burning sensation. It felt a lot like it did when I used Icy Hot, at the point when the icy sensation goes away and leaves nothing but heat—except over every inch of my body.

I nudged Wait. "Hey, man, it's really hard to breathe."

Wait leaned over me. "Okay, open your mouth. Have you got anything in there?"

Kenny looked over Wait's shoulder. "Did you swallow a tooth or something?"

"No." I probed my mouth with my tongue, to make sure all my teeth were still attached. They were, so I grinned at my guys. "I'm good."

I found out later that what had happened was that the concussion of the blast had collapsed my right lung; that's why my breathing had become so difficult and painful. All I knew at the moment was I was having trouble breathing, but I wasn't really panicked about it. I lay really still and thought, *I don't feel like I'm gonna die . . . I'm not gonna die.*

I think that if you're in this kind of situation and you're gonna die, you just know that you're going to die. I never had that feeling. I was sure I was gonna be all right. At the same time I didn't want to take any chances, so I told myself, *Yeah, it hurts, and it's hard to breathe, but just keep goin' through the motions. A little air is better than no air.*

I took small breaths, short gasps, whatever I could, and I just kept on doing that. Then I said to myself, *Stay awake! Keep talkin' to these guys. If you stay awake, keep breathin', and keep talkin', you're gonna be fine.* So that's what I did.

I think one of the big reasons I didn't bleed out was that the bomb that hit my truck was an EFP (explosively formed penetrator). Any explosion—grenades, bombs, mortars, anything—blows up and out. An IED unleashes so much energy that it just goes in every direction. An EFP takes that energy and harnesses it and makes it all go in one direction, or just a few directions. EFPs are made with a cement cylinder roughly five inches in diameter that is closed on one end. It's filled with explosives and then the open end is covered with a metal plate. They get like five of these EFPs, and they stick them close together, all aimed upward, each at a slightly different angle, so that when they explode they unleash a wall of energy. Instead of blowing up and out, all its force goes wherever the EFP was aimed.

The insurgents used to pack their IEDs with plastic explosives—Semtex, C4, whatever they could get their hands on—and then they'd throw in nails, broken glass, rocks, ball bearings, anything they could get. Then they'd cover them with copper plates. When one blew up, all that energy slammed into its plate, which got so hot that it liquefied instantly.

That superheated liquid metal was what pierced my truck's armor. It didn't punch a hole; it *melted* one. At the same time, as that jet of molten copper cut off my legs and hand, it cauterized the wounds, which stopped a lot of the bleeding and gave me a fighting chance to survive. I don't want to take any credit away from Wait, because he did an amazing job, but he'd have had a much harder time keeping me alive if my femoral arteries hadn't been seared shut.

Another bit of luck was that if I'd been driving any faster, I and everyone else in my truck that day would be dead. The reason why has to do with how that IED had been set.

At some point prior to the explosion, one of our tanks rolled over that road's median strip and crushed its curb. When the Iraqis saw that, one of them must have thought, *Oh, that looks like a good place for a bomb.* So they swept it out, measured it, got the dimensions, built a bomb to fit that space, plastered over it, painted it, and set it into that section of the median, so that as we were driving along, it all looked like one long curb.

To trigger it, there had been an invisible laser beam across the street. The Iraqis used lasers or hard-line command-detonation systems because our trucks were outfitted with Warlock systems, multifrequency jammers that block every radio-detonator frequency within a 250-yard radius around the vehicle so that no one can remote-detonate any IEDs.

The way laser detonators worked was that the Iraqis would have a spotter watch a road. After all the civilian traffic had passed—remember that we had 250-yard buffers between us and other traffic in both directions—the spotter would activate the laser sensor, which would shoot a steady, invisible beam across the road. The Iraqis usually set their laser detonators to go off after five clicks, but it could be more or less, depending on what vehicle they were aiming for. Most U.S. convoys in Iraq consisted of three to five vehicles, but we always had at least three. We never went anywhere with fewer than three teams.

My truck had been the last vehicle in the convoy that morning. The IED that hit us had been set to detonate on the fifth click. Each truck would cause two clicks—one when it first broke the beam, another when it cleared the beam. So, the first truck rolled by: *click-click*. The second truck went by: *click-click*. Then my truck's front tire hit the beam: *click-BOOM*.

Here's the catch: the bomb's timer had been primed with the assumption that it would be aimed at a vehicle traveling roughly thirty-five miles per hour, but I had been driving at barely five miles per hour, so my truck was hit while still shy of the bomb's optimal kill zone.

It still did some awesome damage, though: the whole front of my truck looked like it had been ripped apart by a giant can opener.

You want to know what's really ironic about my story?

One of the things I love most in life is speed. I love to drive fast, that sensation of acceleration. But on October 23, 2005, driving slowly saved my life and the lives of my friends.

Go figure.

When the medevac chopper came, it was actually kind of amazing. The pilot had been told not to land there because our position was between an overpass, a building, and some high-voltage electrical lines. But the pilot said, "This kid is dead if we don't land." He set his bird down on the street with barely a foot of clearance in each direction. My guys laid themselves over me so the rotor wash wouldn't drive any more dust and dirt into my wounds.

The next thing I remember was bouncing on the stretcher as I was carried to the helicopter. Once we got inside the helicopter, I looked up at medic and said, "Man, it's really hard to breathe. I need some air."

"All right, man. Hold on—let me lock you in." He lowered the hood over my stretcher, and I heard the locks click shut. Then he looped an oxygen line over my head and stuck the two little tubes up my nose.

As the oxygen kicked in, I began to feel comfortable enough to start letting go. I exhaled and relaxed because I knew I was going for a ride. That's when I finally passed out.

I'd survived being blown up—but as I was about to learn, that had been the easy part.

2

IF YOU'RE NOT FALLING,
YOU'RE NOT TRYING

In the minutes immediately following the explosion that hit my Humvee, I had been aware of what had happened to me—very aware. I had expected to wake up in a Baghdad ER to some doctor asking me a bunch of dumb questions ("Are you in any pain?"), but I didn't.

I awoke to a familiar face looking down at me. My eyes went wide. "Mom?"

Then I did a double take, and I was both surprised and pissed off—what moron had flown my mother into a war zone? "Whoa," I said. "Mom, what're you doing here?"

"No, it's okay," she said. "You had an accident."

"Yeah, I know I had an accident! What the hell are you doing here? You're not supposed to be here!" I'd said that because I thought I was still in Baghdad.

Mom talked fast to cut me off and calm me down. "No, no, no. It's seven days later, and you're in Washington, D.C., at Walter Reed."

I blinked. "What?" It took a few seconds for it all to sink in. "Wait a second—I'm in the United States?" Mom nodded. "You mean I don't have to sit through a seventeen-hour flight home?" I was so relieved that I almost laughed. "That's *awesome*."

I was all drugged up, so it really was a blur, but I knew I was home, and I was alive.

While I was still confined to a bed and even before I'd started my rehab, my mom said to me, "You know you have basically two options here, right?"

I said, "Yup—move on, or roll over and die."

She looked me in the eye and said, "And you're gonna . . . ?"

"I'm movin' on," I said, surprised she even had to ask the question.

My mom told me that when she had received "the phone call" from the Army, she had started crying and looking at my dad, Jim, and my younger sister, Briana, but she had been unable to speak and tell them why. Whoever had called had told Mom exactly what had happened to me, but when she had tried to explain it to my dad and my sister, she couldn't. She'd started making a chopping motion with her hand against her thigh.

She simply couldn't say the words.

My dad grabbed the phone and took over the conversation. After it was done, he had to call everyone—our family and friends—to break the news, because Mom just couldn't talk about it. It was as if the news had cut her heart out.

That changed when she and my family got to Walter Reed.

They were all there when I arrived—my mom, my dad, my brother and sister. The first time they saw me, I was still unconscious. I know they cried when they saw what had happened to me, but I never heard it, and that was because of my mom. She made everybody promise, including herself, that no one would ever cry in front of me.

"Stay strong," she said to them. "If you need to cry, leave the room." She knew I was going to have a hard time in the months to come, and she wanted nothing but positive energy around me. The last thing I was going to need was an excuse to give in to self-pity.

My brother and sister stuck around for the first couple of weeks, which was as long as they possibly could before having to go home and get back to work and school. My dad was with me for four months. His coworkers had all pulled together to donate time off for him to stay that long. It was a huge deal for me, because I really needed him there with me. But my mom—she gave up her job and lived with me the entire time I was at Walter Reed—thirteen months.

At first, they all took shifts because I was in the ICU and it was touch and go at first. My mom and whoever else was in town at any given moment—aunts, uncles, cousins—were at my bedside during the day.

Night was the hardest time for me, though. I never wanted to be alone at night, because I wasn't sleeping very well. To make sure I had company, my dad or my brother slept during the day and sat up with me through the night. Someone had to stay awake because I always had some kind of problem—I was too hot, or I was too cold, or I'd want to shift position but couldn't move. So my dad or Bobby was there to wipe the sweat from my face, or fix my blankets, or do whatever was necessary to make me as comfortable as I could be.

My mom made a point of handling all the paperwork that came with my stay at Walter Reed. Thanks to her, I don't think I ever had to fill out a single form. All I ever had to do was scribble my signature a few times when she put a piece of paper in front of me.

Mom also took care of getting me whatever I needed, whether it was little things like cigs or Pepsi, or big things, like doing all the stupid paperwork and making sure I snagged the first available spot in the Malone House, which is like a hotel for long-term rehab patients at Walter Reed.

You see, the Malone House is always in demand. It's better than being stuck in the hospital, and you get a private room. Its spaces get booked so quickly that a lot of people, if they aren't lucky, end up at the Fisher House, which has less privacy because it's communal living, or off campus at a regular hotel until a space opens up in Malone.

My mom wasn't satisfied leaving our situation to luck. The moment she heard that someone was moving out of the Malone House, she finagled a way for that space to be assigned to me and her. She had us moved in there before anyone else knew the room was vacant.

We lived together in that shoe box of a room for the next year, sleeping on adjacent twin beds. She took care of me, cooked me dinner every night, and kept me company. But most of all, she kept me strong, emotionally speaking.

I started therapy each morning around eight or nine, and I usually got back to my room around three in the afternoon. My mom knew she didn't need to be with me at every therapy session, so she didn't go every day. But if I needed help, or if it was a day where something new or exciting was going to happen, at those times she was always there.

It was the rest of the time, the afternoons and evenings after therapy, when I needed her most. She kept me company so I didn't go stir-crazy. We watched a lot of television together. Well, the truth is, I didn't get into all the shows my mom liked to watch, so eventually I bought a small flat-screen TV and put it right next to the other set. There'd be nights she'd watch one show and I'd be sitting down next to her watching another show on the small set. So I guess technically we *were* watching TV togther.

The loss of movement from my injuries, the cramped room, the daily grind of physical therapy . . . it shrinks your whole world down to just a couple rooms and the same exercises over and over and over. My mom was my connection to the real world. She made sure I got out of the room and out to the mall, or anywhere outside, so that I'd remember there was more to life than our room and the rehab clinic.

Sometimes, when you're dealing with something major, whatever it is—an illness, a relationship breakup, work problems, whatever—it's easy for it to take over your whole life. It's everything you do, talk about, and think about. Your world starts shrinking until that problem is all that's left. Now, I'm not saying you should ignore your problems, not do the things you need to do. But you have to remember there's so much more to life. There's a great big world out there, and you want to be part of it. Laugh with your friends, spend time with your family. Just get out among people . . .

even if it's just going to the mall or sitting in the park watching kids play. Yeah, you may be dealing with some heavy stuff, but don't let it take over your world.

My mom and I joked a lot, and we laughed a lot. That was important. Dealing with your own injuries, and being surrounded by others facing the same problems, can get you down; you can start to lose hope. It's no different for anyone who's had a setback and is struggling to recover. You have to keep your spirits up to go on fighting back toward a normal life. So Mom and I did things together. One time I bought an espresso machine, and we spent an evening trying to reinvent the caramel macchiato. Instead I blew the top off the machine and made a mess out of the whole room— and we both thought that was hysterical.

Another time, I ran my power chair smack into the wall.

Mom made a "tsk-tsk" sound and smiled. "Honey, you're supposed to signal first."

One night, we were lying in our beds and watching *CSI* on television. We used to watch that show a lot. During a commercial break, I said, "Mom! I could play one of those dead people! How cool would that be?"

She turned her head to look at me. "I don't think I would enjoy seeing you like that, but you're right—that *would* be cool. If you want to be a stuntman, you should. You can do anything you want. You just have to work hard, go for it, and see where it takes you."

(A couple of years later, I went for it. And behold—I wasn't just a dead body; I was a living, breathing murder suspect on *CSI: NY*. Being there and playing that role was a profound moment for me. Standing on the set, I thought back to that moment in the Malone

House, years earlier, when I had told my mom that I wanted to be on the show, and she was right there to tell me that I could.)

Mom's faith in me made me believe there was no reason I couldn't do anything. Thanks to her, instead of wasting time wondering what I can or can't do, I spend my time thinking about what I do or don't *want* to do.

Back then, though, I was still kind of sore—everything felt really raw. It's not that I was in constant pain, but my body was a lot more sensitive than it was before or has been since. Even a simple bump or impact would hurt like hell. As a result, I wasn't as quick to jump into action or try new things as I normally am.

I was also kinda raw emotionally. I had to relearn how to do everything. There were things my head knew how to do, but my body couldn't. I'd get frustrated and angry. Sometimes I thought it would just be easier not to try.

My mom didn't plan on letting me get used to sitting on my ass, though. She told me, "You need to keep moving. I know it hurts right now, but the more you work, the faster you'll get used to it." At first I didn't believe her, but she kept telling me that, day after day. And you know what? Pretty soon it started to sink in. I began to get the message.

If someone tells you the same thing over and over and over again, after a while you're going to start to believe it. If you surround yourself with positive people who push you to be your best, and who tell you everything will be all right, it can build you up and keep you going. But if you let yourself listen to people who fill your head with negativity, with pessimism, it won't be long before you start thinking like they do.

The same thing applies to the things you say about yourself. If you call yourself an idiot, or a klutz, or say you're not attractive, pretty soon you'll start believing your own bad press. You owe yourself better treatment than that. Don't put yourself down—there are more than enough jerks in the world who will be happy to do it for you. I'm not saying lie to yourself. I don't want you to stand in front of a mirror mumbling, "I'm good enough, I'm smart enough, and gosh darn it, people like me." I'm just saying give yourself a break once in a while. Don't be so hard on yourself. Imagine a good friend of yours was in your position. What would you say to him? Would you criticize him? Knock him down? No, of course not. You'd encourage him, support him. Well, you deserve the same for yourself.

There were times I forgot to give myself that break, but my mom was there to do it for me. "Your life's not over," she told me. "You can do a lot of things. You're going to get better and move on, and someday soon you're going to do great things." Because my mom kept saying this, not only did I start believing it, other people started believing it, too. It was like a snowball rolling down a mountain, getting bigger by the second, until it got so big and so obvious that you can't stop it.

It became true.

Some people asked how I could put the explosion behind me and move on like that, with no self-pity. I told them I used to be a gymnast, and before that I played baseball; I was an athlete. What happens to an athlete when they get hurt? What do they do? They rehab their injuries, they work to get better, and then they get back in the game.

In my eyes, this was the same thing. My dreams hadn't changed. My goals hadn't changed. Who I was hadn't changed. I got hurt, and I knew I needed to get myself back to the point where I could live on my own and go back to being who I knew I was. I needed to move on, so that's what I told my body to do: *Just get yourself back to good.*

When I first started rehab—maybe for the first four weeks—I would go to therapy one or two hours a day. I'd do occupational therapy to learn how to use my new hand and then I'd do physical therapy to work on my range of motion, stretching, strength training—they were just trying to build me back up a little before they tried to get me walking.

My goal at first was to just get on prosthetics, to see how they felt, to see if I could walk. Once I got on them I was like, "Okay, I can do this." My goal at that point was to find my limits, to push myself to the point where I would fall down. I swear, I must hold the record for falling down at Walter Reed.

My mentality was, "I may be fucked up now, but I'm gonna get better and get back to my life." I just wanted to get this done so I could move on.

The hardest part of rehab—for me, at least—was to really *accept* what had happened to me, but I knew that it was the only way I'd ever be able to go forward.

During my time at Walter Reed, I noticed a major difference between the people who had accepted their circumstances and moved on and those who were still in denial. You could tell who was who based on which people were making steady progress in their rehab and which ones weren't. There were people who were always complaining, making excuses, and just hating life, and they had a lot of trouble in therapy. And then there were others who were just doing it. I honestly believe that the difference was all about who had or hadn't learned to live with what had happened to them.

I don't think there was one moment when I magically went from struggling with acceptance to acceptance. I don't even think you realize it until you're there.

I know what helped me a lot was being around another triple amputee, Joey Bozik; seeing him walking and doing things made me think I could do it, too. But what also helped was small acts of confirmation that showed me I was getting better. I remember one time, I was in the gymnasium at Walter Reed and a couple of guys were throwing around a basketball, and I wondered if I could handle the ball and shoot like I used to. I was just outside the free-throw line and I grabbed the ball, threw it, and made the shot. At that moment, I thought if I could do this, just think what I could do if I really tried and practiced. Something as small as making that basket gave me hope and kept me moving forward, propelling me to my next accomplishment.

Bad things happen to us. It's a fact of life. No one's immune. Sooner or later, we all end up on the shit end of a stick. For me, it was getting blown up; for someone else, it might be losing a job, or a loved one dying, or a house burning down. There are things we can't avoid, at least not forever. We can't always control what happens to us. The only thing we *can* control is how we react to it. We can choose to lie down and die, or we can choose to go on living.

I'm not saying you can or should brush off everything life throws at you. There's nothing wrong with grieving for the friends and family we lose, or with taking time to adjust to major life-changing events. But it's not healthy to mourn forever. Life is meant to be lived forward, and you can't do that if you spend all your time looking backward. You can carry some of that old stuff with you, but don't let it slow you down. At some point you just have to get back on your feet and go. Walk if you have to, run if you can.

I started rehab as soon as I was able because I hate just lying around.

Now, I won't bullshit you: learning to walk on prosthetic legs was a bitch. They felt unnatural to me. And, of course, you don't really feel them, only against your thighs. It's like trying to walk when your legs are asleep. Everyone knows how little control you have trying to walk on numb legs.

I couldn't help but think of Lieutenant Dan Taylor, the soldier Gary Sinise played in *Forrest Gump*, who also lost both legs and finally got prosthetics. But I skipped over the troubles he had before making peace with his situation and went straight for the new legs. When I first started using "Lieutenant Dan" legs, I wanted to know what my limitations were and where my point of no return was. I *needed* to know how far I could go: How far can I lean back? How far can I bend forward? What happens if I stand on one foot? What if I get bumped?

To find out, I actually asked people to try to make me fall. I would close my eyes and say to my therapist, "Push me in some direction. Any way you want." And she would either shove me backward or forward—not hard enough to knock me over, just a nudge to make me need to correct my balance. When that happened, I'd clench anything I could get hold of and try to keep myself upright. One of the biggest things I had to learn was that my instincts in that case were wrong. I was fighting something natural, something I used to deal with without even thinking about it. What would normal people do in that situation? They would just take a step. I had to relearn that and teach my reflexes, *Put your foot out! Take a step! If you're falling left, step left!* I needed to be more active and just push ahead. It's the difference between slamming on the brakes and steering into a skid. You can go in the ditch or you can take control of the situation.

Sure, sometimes I fell. We all do. And I don't just mean people with prosthetic legs. Every one of us falls sometimes, but that means we're pushing ourselves, trying to increase our abilities. You know how people say they fell flat on their face when they've screwed up something they're trying to do? Well, that's what I was doing . . . literally. And that's when I cooked up my motto: "If you're not falling, you're not trying." Someone who never tries something new might not ever fall, but they sure aren't going to do anything exciting either.

The first time I asked my physical therapist to try to push me over, she refused. I expected her response because it was only my first time on "shorties"—prosthetics just a few inches tall; you start on the shortest possible legs and work your way up as you learn how to control them and keep your balance. Because I used to be a gymnast, though, I had great balance. My therapist put the short-ies on me. I stood up and looked up at her. "Now what?"

She shot me a confused look. "Weird—you're not even holding on to anything."

I shrugged. "Am I supposed to be?"

She looked me over and then walked toward me. "Hold on a second." She put her fingertips on my chest and nudged me. I leaned back an inch or so, and then I straightened up. (I didn't take a step because I hadn't learned how to do that yet.) Then she gave me a push forward, and I did the same thing in the other direction. We went side to side, and each time I came up straight and steady. She nodded. "That's pretty impressive for your first time on new legs."

Next, I waddled around, walking and shuffling and doing whatever I could. I had two canes to help me stay upright. I wandered over to a guy who was trotting around with a harness for support and said to him, "Okay, dude, let's go! You and me!"

He just looked at me for a moment, then smiled, and we were off. I tried to move my feet as quickly as I could, and I fell face-first—*splat*. As soon as I hit the floor, my therapist pulled out a piece of paper: an incident report form. She told me she had to fill one out every time a patient falls in therapy.

I just laughed. "Yeah, well, you're gonna have to get a *lot* of those!" She looked at me like I was crazy. I added, "It's really not a big deal. I fell in gymnastics all the time. I'd just get right up and go on. It's no big deal, and I don't know why you guys think it is."

She tried to explain it to me, but the rule still made no sense. I mean, falling was just a part of learning, whether walking on new legs or skating or skiing for the first time. I'll give her an A for effort, though—she tried for a while to keep up with me, but I fell a lot. After a while she just stopped doing the reports.

Soon, after falling a few dozen times a day, I started making real progress with my therapy. That was when my therapists started asking, "What are your weaknesses? What are your strengths? What are you comfortable doing? What are you *not* comfortable doing?"

I thought about that. "Well, I'm comfortable walking uphill. I'm comfortable strolling around inside the clinic."

"Well," they said, "we need to get you outside. We need to get you comfortable in real-life situations." Then they told me, "Walking downhill is really hard." They were right. The therapy clinic is perfectly flat, perfectly level, smooth, and not very crowded. That's not how the world is.

"All right," I said to one of my therapists, "let's work on that. If you see me walking around the clinic, every once in a while come up and shoulder-bump me. Walk into me like we're in a crowded place."

This was important, because in the real world, people don't always realize I need extra space. Even though I wear shorts most of the time—and the reason I do that is so people can see I have prosthetic legs and maybe give me a little room—not everybody sees or notices that I have C-legs. When I go to a crowded place— a mall, a ball game, or whatever—people might bump into me, thinking I'm just an ordinary guy. I knew I'd need to know how to handle that. Kind of like someone taking self-defense classes or maybe learning first aid. You might not be looking forward to the situation, but if something bad happens it's good to be prepared. Having my therapist push my limits on a daily basis is how I learned to just react—and after losing my legs, it was a skill I had to learn all over again, as if I'd never walked before.

Relearning stuff like that—stuff we take for granted—is a lot of work, and not everybody is up for it at first. Starting over from scratch with stuff you've been able to do all your life is a pain in the ass. It's frustrating in a way that learning something new just isn't. There was this one girl at Walter Reed who I heard grumble,

"I swear to God, if I fall off these prosthetics, I'm ripping them off and I'm never getting back on 'em."

That was the stupidest thing I'd ever heard. I couldn't believe she said that. What was she thinking? That they were magic legs? Did she think she'd get it right away? Without having to work for it? No, of course not. That's insane. If I could go back in time, I'd tell her, "If you ever want to walk again, you'd better get ready to fall at least a thousand times, because that's the only way it's ever gonna happen."

Falling on your face isn't easy, and picking yourself up over and over again is even harder. It helps to have a good reason to get up and keep going. Some folks want to win a race or break a record, get better at a sport or an activity, recover from an injury or an illness so that they can enjoy life again, or because people they care about are counting on them.

As far as I'm concerned, any reason that gets you back on your feet and ready to fall again is a good one, and you should hang on to it for as long as you can, and let it take you as far as possible toward your goal.

I woke up in Walter Reed on October 30, 2005, and I was discharged from the hospital roughly six weeks later, on December 14. During that time I'd had more surgeries than I could count, and I'd received more than 120 units of transfused blood.

The first month was the hardest. To extract all the shrapnel from my torso took more than one operation. When I first woke up, my chest and my gut seemed mostly fine. But after one of the follow-up surgeries, I woke up with my abdomen still open and my gut swollen like a basketball. I learned that when surgeons cut through your abdominal muscles and pull everything out, they can't just shove it all back in when they're done—it's not that easy. Your abs hold stuff in place. To give the muscles they'd cut a chance to heal, they put in a black rubber thing that helped keep all my insides roughly where they ought to be, and then over a few weeks they slowly cinched my gut closed, a few millimeters at a time.

After I left the hospital, I was still living on the Walter Reed campus while I started my rehab. Normally, learning to walk on prosthetic legs is a long, slow process. First, you have to let your wounds fully heal. Then you need to be fitted, and after that you start retraining your muscles. It's awkward as hell, and it hurts even more than you think.

A bilateral amputee like me—a person who has lost both their legs—starts rehab by learning how to walk on shorties. You can't do much on shorties except waddle around like a penguin, but you have to master them before you can graduate to taller legs. From shorties you move up to ten-inch legs, and then a slightly taller pair, and after that you finally get full-size legs and start learning to walk again.

Most bilaterals need two weeks, give or take, to get through each stage and move up to the next one. Going from shorties to full-size C-legs is usually a two-month process.

I decided to do it all in one week.

My unit was coming home that January from their tour in Iraq, and I got it into my head that I was gonna be there in Fort Hood, Texas, to greet them when they got off the plane. My doctors didn't think it was a good idea for me to travel so early in my rehab. They were worried I'd fall and crack my head open, I guess. They tried to talk me out of going, but I told them I didn't give a shit about what was happening with me, or how hard I'd have to push myself, because one way or another I was gonna be standing there when my unit came home.

"Look," I said to them, "I was a gymnast. I have balance. Trust me—I can *do* this."

I rushed, I crushed, and I fell on my face about a thousand times. I didn't care how many times I fell, because I knew I needed to accept the falls in order to learn at the pace I wanted. For an entire week, all day every day, I worked my ass off, going from shorties to ten-inchers in record time. I didn't care how many bruises it cost me, because I knew it would be worth it. It was great that I had that goal, that I had something to look forward to and focus on. I used the homecoming of my unit to push myself to the limit and beyond. I think some people in rehab just didn't find something in their future to fight toward. And that's something we all need.

Two days before I was supposed to leave, my doctors gave me a pair of full-size C-legs. By the day of my trip, I still couldn't walk in the C-legs, but I could stand.

That'll have to do, I decided, and I flew down to Texas.

My pal Kenny met me in Texas. He was already back in the States because he'd had a hard time recovering from his wounds in Iraq, so the Army had sent him home. Gietzel, on the other hand . . . I felt bad for him because he'd had to stay in Iraq. An ass wound can get you a few days in a bed and light duty on base after it heals up, but it doesn't get you sent home. So poor Gietzel had had to stay behind and finish his tour.

On January 19, 2006, Kenny and I joined the other guys' families in the Fort Hood gymnasium. Kenny stood with me while I sat in my wheelchair, passing the time. We were wearing our DCUs, as we knew the rest of our unit would be.

Someone called out, "They're here!" Buses pulled up outside. Our unit piled out of them and lined up in formation to run inside the gym and be welcomed home. Kenny and I stood up and saluted as our buddies came charging in. They couldn't believe it when they saw us standing there—especially me, with a big-ass smile on my face. Just think about it. The last time my buddies had seen me I was flat on my back being evacked, my blown-away legs and arm in tourniquets, having trouble breathing. Now here it was just a few months later and I was standing there waiting for them as they came home.

After everyone was inside, the national anthem played and a reporter snapped a photo of me and Kenny standing at attention in front of our unit in formation. I love that photo—it captured one of the proudest moments of my life, and for me it was worth a million words.

Looking back, I can't tell you how many times I fell during the week leading up to that day, because it's not important. What is important is that I got to stand, in my uniform, with my friends and my unit, and smile while the national anthem played.

If I'd had to fall a million times to stand up just that once, I'd have called it a bargain.

———————

The cold, hard truth is that getting the hang of a new limb takes time. After getting back from Fort Hood, I kept at it, always pushing myself, always finding some new challenge. Before I left Walter Reed I saw this prosthetic in the lab. The knee looked like a cage with a big shock absorber and a spring inside it. It was really wild looking, and it got my attention right away, so I asked the prosthetics guys, who I'd gotten to know really well, "What's that?"

"Oh, that's the XT-9," one of them said.

"Okay," I said. "What's an XT-9?"

"A snowboarding knee," said the other guy. "Or wakeboarding."

Jackpot, I thought. I couldn't use them then: I could barely walk. But I knew *one day* I was going to go snowboarding.

"Why don't you hook me up with a set of those?"

They nodded. "All right, Bryan. You got it."

It was a year before I got to use them. I was back in Chicago and I went out and bought a snowboard.

I wanted to test the knees and try out the snowboard in a safe place before I got on a slope, so I did my first test of the snowboarding knee in the living room of my apartment.

My brother, Bobby, was there and he watched as I put the snowboard flat on the living room floor. Then I put the boots on, put my legs on, and got onto the board. I clipped in. Then I just stood there for a second, trying to figure out how it felt. It was as if I was standing on real legs, with my knees just slightly bent.

"Okay," I said. "Good start."

I leaned forward and back, perching the board on each edge, and I was able to keep my balance in both directions. Then I gave it a twist, one way and then the other. I had my brother keep his hands up behind my back while I swiveled the board beneath me, to see whether I'd be able to make it turn.

Once I felt as if I'd gotten the hang of it, I said, "I should be able to do this!" I knew I wasn't gonna get it all right away; I knew I was gonna fall. But I was ready to give it a shot.

It was time to leave my living room and go find some snow.

I packed up my gear and headed off to a slope called Raging Buffalo, a small hill about forty miles from my home in Chicago. It's no mountain. The entire hill is only about a hundred yards from start to finish. If I take a deep breath, I can almost spit that far.

It was dark when I arrived at Raging Buffalo. It was a clear night full of stars, and the air was mild. The snow was packed hard. The only way up was a rope lift, which I thought kind of sucked. Then I heard music by Rise Against playing from the PA system on the guard towers; the guy watching over the mountain was listening to one of my favorite bands. I thought that was awesome, because I was listening to the same band's tunes on my iPod. I took it as a good sign that I could do this.

My first time riding my board on snow, I made it all of two feet. Maybe three.

I landed on my ass.

It took me forever to figure out how to get back up the hill so I could try again. The biggest hassle was that when I fell, I needed other people to help me up. I couldn't get back up on my own.

I tried to walk myself upright with my hands, pushing myself up and back, but I couldn't get all the way to a standing position doing that, and I couldn't just snap myself straight. It's important to be straight when you're on a snowboard. Your center of balance has to be in the right spot, or you'll be on your back or on your face in no time. So I had to go from a completely bent-over position to straight up immediately, and I just didn't have the strength to pull that off.

My first solution was to grab somebody or something near me and pull myself up. Then I would push off and be back in motion.

But I knew I needed to figure out a way to get up by myself, because sooner or later I was going to fall somewhere when I was alone.

That first night, I fell a lot. My first run, I fell four or five times in a hundred-yard stretch. But I made it down, and I'd gotten the feel of it, even if just a bit.

The second time I went snowboarding, I did a little better. I only fell twice down that hill.

By my third outing, I still fell as many times as I had before, but I had a bit more control. I could turn, and I had started to feel the slope as I was riding it.

That sense of accomplishment was what kept me going. The whole thing was trial and error, but I was making progress, and I knew that I just needed to keep doing it to make more progress. The same thing would be true for anybody. Everyone falls when they learn to ski or snowboard or surf. It wasn't really that different for me. Sure, I had my own extra challenges, but plenty of people have trouble learning to snowboard. Whenever I heard from people who knew about snowboarding, they'd tell me it takes three times on a board before you actually feel as if you're grasping the concept. So I told myself, *No matter what, you need to go three times so that you can at least give this a fair shot.* By the third time, I was saying, *Dude! I'm able to do this! As long as I keep at it, I'm gonna be all right.*

Pretty soon I was so confident that I tried going into the half-pipe—and slammed straight into the wall. I didn't go up it—it was just *BAM!* Dead stop. I dusted myself off and said, "Okay, maybe that's not the best idea." I haven't been back to the half-pipe yet . . . but I will. Count on that. Because I'm a much better snowboarder now.

After my fourth run on Raging Buffalo, I came out to Snö

Mountain in Pennsylvania, a really big mountain. I started learning more quickly because I had a longer slope on which to ride. I started staying upright longer, but I would still fall every now and then. One time I fell backward, and I rolled so far that I almost stood up again. I said, "Whoa!" I'd nearly gotten back on my feet—without even trying!

So I let myself fall on my back. My board was facing the top of the mountain, and my head was downslope. Lying there in the snow, I thought, *Let me try something*.

I did a back roll, like I used to do in gymnastics. I let my board come up over my head, and it pulled me over and popped me straight up. The next thing I knew, I was standing on my board with my mouth hanging open. Then I turned down the slope and kept going.

Just like that, I'd figured out how to get up by myself. These days, whenever I fall while snowboarding, I just do a back roll and land on my board. It's so easy that I no longer need anybody with me. I can tackle any slope I want, totally on my own, whenever I feel like it.

Once you learn how to pick yourself up—whether literally or figuratively—falling isn't such a big deal anymore. But you have to be willing to fall as many times as it takes for you to learn that skill. It won't happen overnight. In my case, a lucky fall is what showed me the way to get up again. That's why I don't worry about falling—it's just another part of my journey.

The bottom line is that falling can be your friend. Don't be afraid of it—*embrace it*.

Then get up and keep going.

3

USE THE TOOLS YOU'VE BEEN GIVEN

I'm not going to lie: When I first started recovering at Walter Reed I was bummed. I mean, I lost my legs and a hand. Obviously I was very attached to my body parts—literally . . . and then I wasn't. My early thoughts were that I wouldn't be able to do everything I wanted to do, that I was limited. (Little did I know how wrong I was.)

My family and friends never treated me differently, never let me slack. They pushed me. They wouldn't do things for me that they thought I should be able to do for myself. And I'm grateful for that.

The worst thing—and I still get this today—is when people see me and assume I'm fragile and can't do things for myself. It pisses me off because I can do everything; I'm completely self-sufficient. And when I need help, I'll ask for it.

Most of the time, instead of getting angry I just show people what I can do. For instance, someone might see me heading for a door and rush to open it for me. But when I'm in my chair I move really quickly and usually can get there first, throw open the door, and blow right through it. Sometimes I might even hold the door open for the person.

I just want people to see me and not my chair. I don't want someone to look at me and assume what I can or cannot do. When people see someone who is differently abled, they shouldn't assume that what they see on the outside is the whole person.

There's this guy I work with who has cerebral palsy. He's strapped into a wheelchair, has leg spasms, and sometimes people have trouble understanding him when he speaks. But this guy is brilliant; he's written five books and is the head of his department. We've gone out to lunch together and the waiter will ask me what he wants. I'm like, "Why are you asking me? Ask him." What I want to say is, "Dude, this guy is probably ten times smarter than you, so don't dismiss him like that."

Look, everyone has limitations, maybe some people more than others, but we all have something. It could be physical—from birth, as a result of an accident, illness, or age. But there are other things, too—mental health or emotional issues, economic disadvantages, educational or skill disadvantages. Look, we're not all created the same. We each have our own strengths and weaknesses. It's what we do with what we've got—or don't have—that really matters.

The way I see it, we can either focus on the things we *can't* do or we can figure out another way to do them. We have to use the tools we have to find ways to do the things we think we can't.

Probably everyone knows someone or has heard of a kid who

had a lot of trouble with schoolwork until the teachers figured out he had dyslexia. Before he was diagnosed with this learning disorder that makes reading difficult, his grades were terrible and maybe he was going to be left back. But once he got the proper tutoring and learned some new skills, he was able to do a lot better and his grades improved. He just needed the tools to overcome his limitations.

Look at me. I've got one hand.

A simple task that most people take for granted but that I now think of as a challenge is dealing with buttons on clothing. It doesn't matter if it's a shirt or a coat: you can't easily fasten or unfasten small buttons with one hand. At least, that's what I used to think, when I was just starting my rehab. Now I can do it easily. So what changed? What changed is the way I approach the problem.

At first, I thought my prosthetic hand was useless for tasks like this, small actions calling for fine-motor skills. Then my therapists gave me a special tool to use for buttoning. It's an easy-to-grip handle with a long, narrow metal loop; you stick it through the buttonhole, hook the button with the loop, and pull the button back through the hole. With a little practice I was able to master this "simple" task once again. That is, until I lost the tool. But this time I wasn't as discouraged. I had found one alternative way to deal with small buttons, and I could find another. Sure, the prosthetic hand wasn't precise enough to manipulate shirt buttons, but my right hand still was. I had to get over my inability to do things the way I used to and accept that I had to learn a new way of getting the job done. And after a bit of trial and error and some practice, I taught myself to manipulate small buttons with my right hand and my teeth.

Once I stopped dwelling on the hand I'd lost and learned to use the tool I'd been given in rehab, buttoning a shirt became a possibility for me again. It's still not easy, but I can do it, and that's what matters.

It's not so hard to fall into the trap of thinking there's only one way to do things. When life makes our old methods impossible, a lot of us just stop trying. I saw guys at Walter Reed who'd lost a leg and decided they would never walk again. Sure, they could have learned to use a prosthetic, but they had it in their minds that they couldn't do it. And you know what? With that attitude, they couldn't.

If you lose a tool that you rely on, it's not an excuse to give up. It's your cue to learn how to use another tool or to change your way of working so you can get the job done with the tools you still have. Most people, if they lost a hand, would just give up and say, "I can't button a shirt." They'd settle for always having someone else help them, and they'd give up a bit of their independence as a result.

I'm telling you right here, right now: *that's not good enough.*

There is always another way. It's your responsibility to find it. It might take trial and error. Try something new. You may fail ninety-nine times, but that hundredth attempt might be the ticket to success.

It might be a matter of thinking of things another way. Instead of thinking about abilities you no longer have, focus on those you do have and see if there's a way to accomplish your goal with them.

Sometimes it might help to talk to someone and get a completely fresh perspective. You might be too close to the situation. The answer might be obvious, but you need a fresh set of eyes to see it.

Sometimes you really do hit a wall, though, and I understand that. My basic prosthetic hand, for instance, has some real limitations. I can't use it to pick up a penny off the ground. I just don't have the necessary fine-motor control in my fingers.

But I have three different kinds of attachments for my left arm. Besides a hand, I have a hook and a gripper. With the hook, I *can* pick up a penny—or a pen, or a book, or whatever. Maybe the hook doesn't look as "natural" as my prosthetic hand, but it's the right tool for the job, so if I need it, I use it. The gripper attachment is the better choice for when I'm handling tools, such as when I'm working on a car.

Just because what I have doesn't look like a natural hand doesn't mean I shouldn't use it. I have to use what I can in order to do what I need to do, and I can't worry about what it looks like.

It's kind of like watching monkeys break open coconuts with rocks. Monkeys don't get self-conscious because they can't rip open coconuts with their bare hands. They hit them with rocks and branches, and they experiment with new ways of busting those things open. They slam them on boulders and do whatever they have to—whatever works. That's what we all need to do in life, no matter what we're dealing with. Find a way. Make new tools out of anything we find and never give up. Find a way to get the job done and break into that coconut.

I bet you wouldn't think a guy with one arm and no legs could do automotive repairs, would you? Well, I can. For my younger sister Briana's eighteenth birthday, I wanted to surprise her by giving her a car. I bought her BMW. Okay, a used 1994 BMW. It ran all right, but there were certain things wrong with it. The interior leather was all messed up, the tires and the rims were nasty, and

45

the headlights and taillights were old and didn't work properly. But it was still a BMW, right?

Then I got a crazy notion in my head: I wanted to make that car like new for her, and I decided to do the work myself. I mean, why not? I have mechanical knowledge. And what I didn't know I could look up. I'm not completely illiterate. I know how to do things and follow directions, and doing the work myself would make the gift more meaningful. It would really be from me and not just from my wallet.

To make sure I wasn't getting in over my head, I planned the whole job before I started. I broke down each task into a series of steps and made sure I knew how I would get them all done. It might sound like a lot of trouble, but once I sat down and figured it all out, I realized it was totally doable. It was just a matter of being prepared. I also knew that if I needed help with any part of it, my dad and my cousin Chris were only a phone call away (and they both pitched in at my request on a few occasions).

The next day I logged on to the Internet and ordered all the parts I needed. A couple of weeks later, after all the parts arrived, I put on my gripper, went down to my garage, and did the work. I jacked up the car and changed all the tires. I brought that car back to life one piece at a time and made it the best it could be, inside and out.

I could tell that I was doing something special. I took my time and made sure it was done right. Let me tell you, it felt good.

What I'm driving at by telling you this is that you need to know about the tools that are available to you. You should know what each one is for, its strengths and weaknesses, what it can and can't help you do. Most important, you should know there's nothing wrong with using them. Some people hit a wall and decide, *If I can't do this the way I used to, there's no point.*

That's ridiculous. There's nothing wrong with the tools at your disposal.

Other people get discouraged when they start learning new ways to do old tasks because the new way takes longer. Well, you know what? It's only going to take you longer the first ten or fifteen times you do it. That may seem like a long time, depending on what you're learning, but we're talking about the difference between being able to do it yourself or having to ask for help for the rest of your life. Fifteen times isn't so bad compared to that. After those fifteen times, it's gonna be like second nature. You just need to be patient and give yourself time to learn.

That's what I'm doing all the time. I'm using whatever I can find to do what I need to do and live the way I want to live. I use everything around me, and if I don't find what I need, I ask other people to help me find or make what I need.

I think I developed this attitude while learning how to fight. In the military—during basic training and again later, when I was learning to be a military policeman—I received instruction in hand-to-hand combat. The U.S. Army teaches soldiers to fight dirty. They teach us to win and make sure we stay alive and get ourselves out of danger, no matter what it takes. That's where I learned to use anything I could get my hands on: chairs, pens, rocks, bottles, dirt—whatever. I was taught to do whatever is necessary to slow down my enemy and gain the upper hand. In a fight, every advantage, no matter how small, is valuable.

Now I apply that same way of thinking to my everyday life. Being a triple amputee, I learned quickly that I had to use the world around me. When I first got into a wheelchair, I thought the only way I could move was to put my hands on top of the wheels and push. Soon I was getting really tired, because it takes a lot of effort to move that way.

One day I was going up a hill. I was fighting for every inch. My hand was rubbed red and raw from pressing on the tires, and my shoulders were killing me. Every push made me feel like I was gonna rip the skin off my palm.

Between gasping for breaths I was muttering, "This sucks!"

Then I looked to my right and saw a metal railing that ran along the sidewalk. At that moment I felt as if something in my mind finally kicked into gear. I looked down at myself, and then I reached for the railing and said, "Wait, let me try this."

I grabbed the railing and pulled myself forward as hard as I could—and I flew nearly twenty feet. It was awesome! Instead of creeping up that hill, I was racing up it. That was all it took to change the way I thought about moving in my chair. *To hell with putting my hands on the wheels*, I decided. *I'm just doing this!*

Since then, I've learned to use my surroundings to my advantage. Every doorway, desk, railing, and countertop I can reach is a tool waiting to be used, and I'm not shy about using them.

One thing you shouldn't do is let your pride stop you from using the tools you need. And don't be afraid to ask for help when you need it. Never worry about looking weak or even foolish. It's a lot dumber to settle for a crappy situation than it is to trust someone to help you when you need it.

Let me give you a perfect example of what I mean. A few years ago, I was in Pennsylvania on one of my visits to the corporate headquarters of Quantum Rehab. I was staying in a hotel. The bathroom in my hotel room was really small, and it wasn't handi-capped accessible. It was just big enough that I could roll my wheel-chair inside and park it in front of the toilet, next to the tub. The sink and mirror were outside, in the main part of the room.

One morning around seven, I rolled into my bathroom so I could take a shower and get ready to go to work. I pulled back the shower curtain, looked up, and saw that the showerhead was turned toward the wall. I shook my head and wondered, *Who does that? Why the fuck would you do that?*

I tried to reach it, but I couldn't—I've got no legs, remember? Fed up, I thought maybe I could live with it. I turned on the shower. The water ran down the wall and into the drain.

I couldn't use the shower like that, not even if I got under it and tried to splash the water onto myself. *Maybe I could work up a lather,* I realized, but how would I rinse it off?

Forget it, I decided. It wasn't working.

I started looking around, searching for a way to fix the problem. After a few seconds, I thought I had cooked up a possible solution. I reached over and put the toilet lid down. Then I lifted myself onto it, turned to face the bathroom door, and hoisted myself up onto the back of the toilet, on top of the water tank.

So far, so good.

My back was against the wall. I stuck my arms out wide to help me keep my balance. The showerhead was above me and to my left. I leaned left and stretched my prosthetic hand toward the shower-head. Then I realized I wouldn't be able to grasp the showerhead with that hand. I was going to need real fingers to do this job. I would have to get my right hand over there.

The biggest problem I had right then was the size of my perch.

The tank of that toilet was so small, so narrow, that if I so much as dropped my head to look down, I was gonna swan-dive right off that thing. Keeping my head up and my eyes forward, I tucked my right hand to my chest and slowly slid it toward my left side.

To be honest, I don't know what I was thinking. I could barely reach the showerhead with my left hand—there was no way I could reach it with my right hand from that position. I must have been really desperate for that shower, though, because I told myself, *Fuck it, just go!*

I went for it. I lunged and made a wild grab for the showerhead.

I fell off the toilet and my shoulder hit the lid on my way down. The impact catapulted me off the seat and onto the side of the tub. My ribs smacked against the edge, and then I flipped and landed on my back inside the bathtub.

For a few seconds I just lay there, looking up at the shower-head . . . and then I started laughing as I asked myself, *Why didn't I just call the front desk?*

I guess I didn't think of it sooner because I had gotten into the habit of always doing things for myself. That moment in the tub became a major learning experience for me. I had taught myself the hard way that it's not always a bad thing to ask for help. When there are people you can reach out to, people whose job it is to help you, don't be afraid to call on them. That's what they're there for. Always look for the simplest answer. Don't think you have to risk taking a header off a toilet when an easier solution is just a phone call away.

I took this lesson to heart and put it to good use not too long afterward, when I got interested in learning to ride quad ATVs (all-terrain vehicles).

The first day I went riding quads in the hills outside Scranton,

Pennsylvania, I was a passenger on the back of a vehicle driven by a guy named Casey. After we'd been driving awhile, we stopped at a place called the Landfill. It's a wide-open area where you can just let it rip really fast. There are all kinds of bumps and dips, so you can jump and stuff.

Another rider, a guy named Marcel, said to me, "Hey, man. My bike's automatic, and it's got power steering, and the brakes are up here by the steering wheel, so you could ride it."

"Really?" I said. "Awesome!"

"You want to take it for a quick spin?"

"Sure!" I hopped onto his quad and figured out pretty quickly how to maneuver it. At the time I was wearing one of my regular prosthetic hands, but I could see that if I had been using a different kind of prosthetic, one fitted with a ball-and-socket-style adapter to keep it locked to the steering wheels, I'd really be able to do this.

So I took a run on the quad. Man, that thing could fly! I loved the thrill of acceleration, that feeling of being right on the edge of danger; it made me feel more alive than I'd felt in months. Every part of it was a rush—the engine's throaty roar, the rich odor of gasoline, the dusty grit on my teeth, and the cool blast of wind in my hair. It was power, speed, and freedom all at the same time. I'd never felt anything quite like it.

At one point, as I was coming off a jump, I got that ATV like six inches off the ground. I was psyched. "All right!" I felt pumped. I knew this was for me.

I was ready to spend some money to make ATVs a part of my life. I was ready to make it work. I wanted to do it, so I knew I would figure out a way to make it happen.

After I bought my own quad and took it out for a ride, I realized,

Hey, I could fall off this thing really easily. One good bump and I could get tossed clean off. I gotta do something about that. To keep myself from ending up as roadkill, I came up with the idea of side pads to hold my hips where they belonged on the seat.

It was a fine notion, but not one that I was qualified to do for myself. Fortunately, I had learned by taking a header off a toilet that I don't need to do everything on my own.

I returned to my office at Quantum Rehab and said to the company's mechanics and engineers, "Yo, I need some paddles on this thing. Something to keep my hips in."

They had me bring the quad to the shop at company headquarters. Once they started working on it, they had a field day. They customized it, made the paddles adjustable, and built the whole thing with spare parts—all on their own time.

What is the moral of this story? Solving problems is all about figuring things out, thinking up solutions, and getting it done. You can sit there and talk about a problem all you want, but nothing's ever gonna get better unless you get off your ass and do something about it. That doesn't mean you have to do everything yourself, though. Telling the right person about your problem at the right time can go a long way toward fixing things. But it all starts with having the drive to stop talking and start doing.

I bet I know what you're thinking. *That all sounds nice, Bryan, but how am I supposed to use this? I've got real problems. How do I find the tools to fix them?*

First, there is no one answer to this question. The tools that work for me might not work for you. We all have our own issues, and that means we all need to make our own solutions. The "tools you've been given" can mean a lot of things. It's not just your natural abilities or your physical attributes. Your friends, your family, the government, your school or college, even a piece of music or a story that means something to you—these are all tools you can use to change your life, directly or indirectly. Getting help from friends, taking advantage of a government program, or taking classes can help you out in short-term or long-term ways. Just listening to some great music can calm you down or cheer you up when you need it most. Even the phone book can be a valuable tool, if you're willing to use it.

Before you decide your problems are impossible to handle, ask yourself some questions, and try to be honest when you answer them:

Have you really done everything you can? Tried every angle? Or did you give up when you started to realize the only options you had left were the ones that required real work? Most of the time if there's more than one course of action open to you, there's a simple way to tell which is the right one: it's the one that will require you to make the greatest effort.

If it's a moral or ethical problem, the easy way out is almost always the wrong way, and the hard way is usually the correct choice. A good rule of thumb in such cases is that going back or around is cheating. The honest paths are forward and through.

Did you ask anyone for help? No matter how many times you hear people tell stories about being "self-made" successes, remember this: no one in this world ever really does anything completely alone. Millionaires and billionaires build their fortunes on the backs of people who pave the roads, lay the train tracks, work on loading docks, run fiber-optic cables, manage the banks, and do thousands of other jobs that too many of us take for granted.

There is no shame in asking for help. Our friends, families, and neighbors often are willing to pitch in, but too often we let pride get in our way. Don't worry about looking weak or stupid. If you muster the courage to ask, I think you'll find the world is full of people who really want to do the right thing and give one another a hand up during tough times.

Sometimes, however, one can end up in a hard place with no one to turn to—no family, no friends, not even trusted coworkers or neighbors. When you have no cash or credit, it can seem like there are no options. Life can feel like little more than a disaster waiting to happen. Maybe this is the jam you're in right now as you're reading this. You feel as if you have no place to go, and you want to ask, "What tools do I have, Bryan?"

You have *yourself.* You are your own most valuable resource.

The best tool of all is courage. A lot of people mistake courage for fearlessness. They aren't the same thing. If you never feel fear, then you're an idiot. Fear is a very important tool: it's a warning of danger. Courage is about mastering your fear, controlling it instead of letting it control you. Being brave is all about having the discipline to do the right thing despite your fear.

Life can take everything from you except your will to keep on fighting, to keep on working to make your life better. The only way to lose that is to give it up, and that's a choice. But even if you've lost the will to fight, you can get it back just as easily: it's just a matter of deciding not to surrender—to not give up. You can choose to take back control of your life.

So, no matter what life is throwing at you right now, this is my advice: *Get up.* Keep going. Find a way to do what you need to do. If you need help, ask for it.

And whatever you do, *don't give up.*

4

WE'VE ALL BEEN HURT

Since recovering from the wounds I suffered in Iraq, I've realized that we all have our issues. Whether it's missing legs, or a lousy job, or not knowing how to pay to send your kid to school, everybody has their own problems—but yours shouldn't consume you or hinder you from moving forward with your life.

It's just a fact of life that bad things will happen to us. Sometimes they happen to a lot of us at once, like in a flood or an earthquake or a tornado. Other times they happen to a few of us, or to one of us, like losing a job, or wrecking a car, or having a house burn down. I've heard so many people in these situations say, "I'm fucked."

When I hear that, I say, "No, you're not. You won't realize this for a few weeks, or months, or maybe years, but in all reality this is gonna be the best thing that's ever happened to you. Now c'mon, let's go figure it out. Let's work through it and get you goin' again."

The ones who choose to get up and go forward, most of the time they find a better job. They build a better house. In my personal experience, every event that I've ever thought of as a tragedy has always worked out for the better. So you know what I tell people?

"It's gonna be all right. Have faith. You'll figure it out. You'll find a way. I promise."

Look, I know this might sound like a bunch of positive-talk bullshit, but I'm not just talking out of my ass. I'm not some guy who's had a charmed life feeding you some line. I'd say I've seen my share of bad things. But I've accepted the bad stuff and just kept moving ahead.

I know that no amount of positive thinking is going to protect you from all the bad things that life can throw at you. You could live in a germ-proof bubble inside a nuclear fallout shelter and you still wouldn't be 100 percent safe—and even if you were, what kind of life would that be?

What matters in life isn't what happens to us but how we choose to react to it. We can mope and stew and complain about how unfair life is, or we can get up and keep going.

To see this idea in action, watch a dog that has lost one of its legs. Having a leg amputated is a major trauma—believe me, I speak from experience—but does a three-legged dog lie down and sulk? No. Within a few days, almost any dog will get up and start teaching itself how to walk again. Dogs don't need pep talks; they don't sit around and feel sorry for themselves. Look into their eyes and you can see their secret: They get up because they *want* to. They fight to move on because it's what comes naturally to them.

We could all learn a lot from dogs.

I believe the single most important factor in whether each of us is happy is how we choose to think about our lives. We make ourselves happy or miserable. Forget about what other people do or say; put aside the things that happen to you. You can't control other people, and you can't dictate terms to fate. The only thing that's up to you is how you react to events.

For instance, many people, when they first hear about my experience in Iraq, want to express sympathy. I tell them, "Don't feel bad for me. Maybe you see what happened to me as a tragedy, but I don't." That surprises a lot of folks. Some of them don't believe me, but it's true. I think of the day I got blown up as just another day in my life; that event is just another thing that happened to me. I don't see it as the beginning of my story as a person, or as the end. It's just a middle chapter, and not even the most important one, in my opinion.

It was a pretty painful part of my life, though. Some days I dealt with the pain fairly well, but sometimes I didn't. For instance, before I got hit, I'd always enjoyed my dreams. They had always been really vivid and sometimes completely crazy. I used to wake up and tell my Army roommate, Crenshaw, about whatever dream I'd just had. He'd always shake his head, grin, and say, "You're messed up, man. You should write these down. You could sell 'em." I wish I had. I bet a few would have made great movies.

After the accident, though, my dreams went bad on me. The first week after I woke up at Walter Reed, my dreams were positively surreal. In one, I felt as if I was sitting up in my bed instead of lying down, and that my legs extended down through the bed and touched the floor. Some nights, I dreamed I was still normal, with all my limbs, as if the bomb had never hit me. Over time, I began to change in my dreams. I started to see myself with prosthetic limbs, but I was still moving around as if I had regular limbs.

It was strange to wake up in the mornings, look down, and not see anything at the end of the bed where my legs used to be. That took some getting used to.

Soon it got to the point where I didn't sleep well in the hospital. I was able to sleep only one or two hours per night. The doctors kept telling me, "You need more sleep. You need to rest so you can heal." It didn't matter what they said. I simply couldn't stay asleep in that place. It might have been all the drugs they were giving me. Come to think of it, maybe the drugs were part of why I had such lousy dreams.

Right after I got out of the ICU at Walter Reed, I stopped remembering my dreams completely. I wake up and don't even remember dreaming. I hardly ever recall my dreams these days, and I don't think I've ever dreamed of myself being in a wheelchair. I know it might seem strange, but I think I miss my dreams as much as I miss my legs and my hand. They were part of me, and now I feel like they're gone. Maybe I should think of it as a trade-off. I may not dream at night, but I'm living plenty of dreams during the day.

One thing that has stayed with me, however, is pain.

I get phantom pains and sensations all the time. There are pills that I take when that happens, but their side effects suck. Part of what makes my phantom pains hard to cope with is that they're unpredictable. I might feel fine for a few days or even a week. Then, when I'm focused on something else—*BAM!* they're back. Even after all these years, I still don't know what triggers them, so I have no idea how to control them. All I can do is grit my teeth, take another fistful of pills, and tough it out.

When I lie down at night in bed, that's usually the worst time for me, because it's so quiet. I have nothing else to think about except the tingling in my nonexistent legs. It starts out as pins and needles. At first it's a distraction, but it quickly gets worse—a lot worse. Before long it feels like daggers and hot pokers jabbing me.

That's not even the worst kind of phantom pain that I get. There are some that last for only a few minutes, but they can be excruciating. Imagine a huge 250-pound man wearing cowboy boots stomping on your toes and grinding them into the pavement. That's what it's like. When those hit, all I can do is bang my leg up and down, hoping and praying that I can smack the nerve that's misfiring and make it stop before I lose my fucking mind.

The doctors told me they don't know what causes these sensations, they have no idea how to make them stop, and that I might have to deal with them for the rest of my life.

"Well," I said after getting the news, "at least I'll never get bored."

When the pain hits, all I can do is remind myself that it's temporary. After it fades, I remind myself that surviving those kinds of moments makes me tougher. I like to think that it's teaching me something—patience, maybe, or perhaps humility or empathy. But sometimes I snap, and I just want to scream at God, "Why are you making me go through this? Haven't I suffered enough already? Don't you think you've made your point yet?"

Then I remember that the key to moving forward in life is learning to accept what we can't change. If I could make my pain go away forever with a snap of my fingers, I would, but that's not an option. Instead, I have to stop pretending that it will go away on its own; I need to stop wishing it away or waiting for it to go away and just find the strength to keep going even though I know the pain will come back sooner or later, no matter what I do. It's not easy to do this. Sometimes it feels like giving up hope, but it isn't—it's simply accepting reality as it is and continuing my journey.

I know it can be hard to lose the things we love, but too many of us measure our lives by the stuff we own—by the value of our houses, cars, clothes, gadgets, and bank accounts—or by the illusion of status that we get from our jobs.

When your things get damaged or destroyed, or when your job is taken away, it can feel as if there's a hole in your life. That feeling of emptiness can be frightening, but I'm telling you it's an opportunity—a chance to replace a job or an object with something that really matters: a relationship, an experience, or an accomplishment. It's a chance for you to grow as a person.

Let's say you've just been laid off from your job. Naturally, your first reactions will be negative. Maybe you're angry because it seems so unfair, or you're nervous because you don't know how you're going to pay your bills. It can also be humiliating; it feels like a badge of failure. You don't want to admit it, not even to yourself, never mind deal with that stack of paperwork down at the unemployment office. All these feelings are natural, but it's up to you to make sure they're also short-lived, because you need to get on with your life.

Adapting to life after losing a job won't be easy. It'll mean making changes. You need to find ways to spend less money—maybe just for a while or perhaps for a long time—and give up some luxuries you took for granted. This probably won't be fun. And the longer you are out of work, the harder it will be. But you have to cut back where possible, keep looking for a new job, and weather this hardship the best you can.

Tough times suck. I'm not gonna lie. But you can't let them knock you down. Besides, what choice do you have? Like my mom told me when I woke up at Walter Reed, you have two choices: You can roll over and die or move forward. Which are you going to do?

And when you talk about losing material things, it should be even less of an issue. A wrecked car is an expensive problem and an annoying inconvenience, but as long as no one is hurt because of it, it's not the end of the world. The same goes for the loss of a house. A house is just a structure, just a place like any other—a *home* is wherever you feel safe; it's where you can be with people you care about.

The worst part of having a home destroyed—whether by fire, flood, tornado, earthquake, or some other disaster—is losing truly irreplaceable things. You can't just go out and buy another old family photo album full of memories. You can never replace your kids' drawings that hung on the refrigerator, or the handmade gifts that remind you of Christmases past. I know that, and I'm not saying not to mourn your losses. And I can't imagine someone not being angry or depressed about that kind of loss at some point. It's only natural to have emotional attachments to those things. But tragic as such losses are, they serve as important reminders to us that things don't last, and neither do we. We're all just passing through this world, and nothing is forever.

I can already hear some of you thinking, *But what about the death of a loved one, Bryan? How do you put a positive spin on that?*

My take on death is kind of funny. I've seen a lot of it.

In combat, I've seen lethal shots miss people, go around people, kill good people, and leave bad people alone. It doesn't matter who you are. You could get struck by lightning. There are a million ways you could die. Freak accidents. Routine accidents. It's so random that I've come to believe that if it's your time to go, it's your time to go.

If we're talking about a death due to old age, I would just tell someone who was grieving, "Hey, this is the way it was meant to be. It was their time. They're in their better place now." There are many possible ways of thinking about death and what it really means, or whether it means anything at all, but my point is that it's not a bad thing. It's part of nature. Everyone passes on. Sooner or later, we all need to move on from this life.

It's inevitable: *everybody dies*. And those left behind need to grieve.

Everyone mourns in their own way. We all need time to process big moments like these. Do what you have to do to make your peace with it, but the important thing is to accept what has happened. You can't undo the past; you have to live with it, to accept what you can't change. If you don't, *you're* going to die—inside, by degrees, a little bit every day.

There's no point being afraid of death or dwelling on it or being angry at it when it takes someone we care about. The key to accepting this part of existence is to *celebrate life*. Don't think about what you've lost when someone dies, but about what you gained from knowing the person. Remember the joy, the wisdom, and everything else good they brought to your life.

Truth be told, being around death doesn't really bother me anymore. I've experienced so much of it, and seen so much of other people dealing with it, and learned so much about myself in the process, that I understand now that I can't change stuff like that.

My own death, though, is a slightly different story. I admit I'm scared of it, if only because all I can think of when I imagine death is *space*—not stars, just blackness. Empty and *going on forever.* What weirds me out is when I try to imagine what "forever" really means. When you die, you're *forever* dead, gone. And that frightens me, just a little.

But . . .

I can't change that.

When I think about this, I understand why we have religion: it offers us hope and gives us ideas we can understand to replace the ones that we can't understand. Now, I don't want to get into a whole thing on religion; there are some things I believe and some I don't, and that's my business. I do have a lot of questions, but I'm more interested in *living my life* than in worrying about my death. I'm not worried about whether there's a God; I'm worried about such questions as *Am I gonna have kids? Who am I gonna marry? What am I gonna do tomorrow? What's for lunch?*

I don't know why we're here. To be honest, I don't think *anybody* really knows that. Nobody knows what life means, or what happens after death, or *anything*. Anyone who tells you they know all the answers is lying, deluded, or trying to sell you something.

One thing we do know is both bad and good things happen to us and the people around us. Seems a pretty simple idea to me that we should at least try to make things better for ourselves and others, to try to have more good than bad. But when the bad is piling on, it's sometimes hard to think about the good stuff. One thing that makes it hard for us to recover after we've been hurt is that sometimes we don't know how to let go of the pain. It becomes part of us, and before long, even though we hate it, we start to cling to it, even if just out of habit. So how do you break free of that?

Sometimes the best way to heal is to continue to give your best even when you don't feel like giving at all. It's similar to the advice some people offer about making yourself smile when you feel depressed. Forcing yourself to put on a brave face can actually make you feel happier. Imagine how much better you might feel if you get up and do something, too.

Part of what makes this attitude work is that when other people see you making the effort, they respect you more. They draw inspiration from you and reflect it back to you as approval. When you feel that good energy coming back, it's like a reward—and it all started with you putting out good vibes in the first place. I guess what I'm talking about is something like karma: the idea that if you do good things, good things will happen to you. If you project positive energy into the world, you'll create a feedback effect and get it back multiplied.

The most important thing is to not give in to negative energy. Don't surrender to bad feelings. It's not wrong to feel bad, but you shouldn't let dark emotions take over your life. If this seems too touchy-feely for you, look at it from a more selfish angle: when you're stewing in anger or wallowing in depression, do you feel good? No, you feel like shit. When you're pissed off you mess up your stomach, you drive up your blood pressure, and you make your face look all scary. When you get depressed you bleed away all your energy and look like a basset hound.

You deserve better than that, and so do the people around you.

There are many reasons why people make the wrong choice in

situations like this. Sometimes it's the result of fear; sometimes it's just laziness. The truth is, it's easier to coast along than to change direction. Pretty soon people get used to being sad or angry or pitied, and then that becomes their way of life. Once this happens, it gets even harder to change, because lots of people are afraid of change, even when it's for the best.

So how do you shake off bad feelings? Do whatever it takes, whatever works for you. Some folks just need to go out and do something fun. Other people say the key is to do something nice for someone else, some random act of kindness to get you thinking about other people instead of about yourself. When I'm in a bad mood, I know that I can cheer myself up by listening to some really kick-ass music, songs that make me feel like Superman.

Only you can know what will work for you, and it's your job to seek it out. After all, if you fell into the ocean you wouldn't just let yourself sink, would you? No, you'd look for the light, then you'd start kicking and fighting to get back to it. This is the same thing.

You're stronger than you think you are, trust me. I know that "normal" can seem like it's far away when you feel like shit, but the only way to get back there is to work for it.

The good news is that once you start the journey, each step will get easier. It's like physics: objects at rest tend to remain at rest, and objects in motion tend to remain in motion.

Life is about forward motion. So get moving, already!

5

GIVE IT ALL

When I was growing up, my mom always told me, "Do things right the first time and you won't have to do them again." Actually, she told me a lot of things, but most of the time I wasn't paying any attention to her. I was off in my own little world half the time, goofing around with my brother or whatever, and like most kids I thought I knew everything. The reason I remember this particular example of motherly wisdom will become obvious soon enough.

I grew up in a small town called Rolling Meadows, a suburb northwest of Chicago, with my identical twin brother, Bobby, and my mom. My mom and my biological father divorced when Bobby and I were four. My mom eventually remarried a man I will always consider my dad and they had my sister, Brianna, when Bobby and I were eleven, but for those first years after my mother and father divorced, it was just me, Bobby, and Mom, so our mom had to work to support us. The first place I remember living was a huge apartment complex. There were twenty-five buildings, and each one contained anywhere from ten to twenty condominiums. There were tennis courts, swimming pools, and a huge common green in the middle of it all. It was nice, despite being on the edge of a ghetto full of gangs.

Growing up with an identical twin brother, I never had to look far for something to do or for friends—I was born with a best friend. Bobby and I were the type of kids who would get home from school, throw our book bags down, and shoot right out the door. We'd come back in time for dinner, and then we'd race outside again until curfew. You couldn't keep us indoors. We were very outgoing, very athletic, and always wanted to get our hands dirty.

There were dozens of other kids living in the complex, so Bobby and I always had someone to play with. Sometimes, on summer nights, all the kids would come out, and we'd divide into two equal groups and take turns chasing one another all over the place.

O'Hare International Airport was very close by, and we lived right in the path of its landing pattern, so sometimes we'd try to race low-flying aircraft from one end of the complex to the other. We were always too slow. On the few occasions when we thought we'd beat the planes, it was only because they were flying so high overhead that they seemed to be moving in slow motion.

One kid, Josh Kozma, was my and Bobby's best friend. He's a Marine now. Back then we liked pretending to be FBI agents. We'd use masking tape to write "FBI" on the backs of our blue windbreakers and "patrol" the complex on our bicycles. One time we actually pulled over an old lady for blowing through a stop sign. It might seem crazy, but she actually stopped and played along with us—she even let us write her a ticket.

Why am I telling you all this? It's not just some detour down memory lane, I promise. The point of this is to get you thinking about how much heart and energy we all used to put into games when we were kids. Sure, it was just make-believe, but at the time it seemed vitally important, so we threw ourselves into it with everything we had. We gave it our all.

Somewhere along the way, as we get older, we stop doing that. Eventually, some of us forget how. We learn to go along to get along, to take the easy way out, to do the bare minimum.

As a teenager, I took the easy way out of everything. "Clean your room," my mom would say, or "Do the dishes," or "Rake the leaves." I never did a great job. I always skipped a bit that I shouldn't have, or I left some part of it undone. I think it was because I just didn't care.

Prime example: It used to be my job to clean the bathroom in our house, every Sunday. It was a chore in every sense of the word, and it was always the last thing I wanted to do. Whenever I finally got around to it, I'd push a rag around the tub, wipe it once across the countertop, and do whatever I could to get out of there as quickly as possible so that I could go play with my friends or just do whatever I wanted—as long as it wasn't cleaning that bathroom. You could kind of tell I'd been there, but let's just say the porcelain never gleamed, and the chrome never sparkled.

Then my mom would step inside the bathroom, see what a lousy job I'd done, and say to me, "You call this clean? Do it again."

Busted, I would start over, grumbling under my breath. I spent half of every Sunday redoing stuff I'd done wrong. If I'd done my job correctly in the first place, I would have had twice as much free time to enjoy myself. Not that I wanted to hear that when I was fourteen. And now you know why I remember just that one bit of advice. It just took me a long time to really understand it.

When I was a kid, I blew off my homework, or else I did a sloppy job and called it "good enough." I never realized how intelligent I was until after I left school. Then, one day, I looked around and realized, *Hey, I'm not a moron. I can learn about anything. I can do whatever I want.* It would be easy for me to blame someone else for the lateness of this discovery. I could say my teachers never pushed me to excel, or my mom didn't pay enough attention to my homework, or any of a hundred other excuses. The truth is that there is only one person to blame for my shoddy performance in school, and that's me.

Nowadays I take pride in the things I do. I *want* to give my all. I want everything I do to be good. I don't want people to look at my work and say, "Oh, that's lame. He was just phoning it in. He doesn't give a shit." I don't want to let anybody down. More important, I don't want to let myself down. So you know what? Everything that I do, I make it top-notch. If I commit to do something, I'm going to do it to the best of my ability. If I set out to clean my bathroom, I want it *spotless.* I don't want it teenager clean, I want it *clean. My* clean.

A lot of my attitude adjustment about what constitutes "clean" came from being in the Army, but the basic lesson applies to everything. I admit that I haven't always given the Army its due. If you'd asked me right after I got blown up what I owed to the Army, I'd probably have said, "Fuck the Army. It's bullshit." But the truth is that the Army taught me to give my life structure. I learned how to take care of myself in any situation, how things are supposed to work, and how to be an *individual*. Being in the Army gave me self-confidence and taught me how to lead people. Many skills that I think of as essential in my life, I learned from being in the military.

Most of all I learned what it means to commit to something. For instance, if you decide to go snowboarding, don't go to the top of a mountain just to bitch, "Oh, it's cold, my feet hurt," or just go down the mountain one time and say, "Okay, I'm done." What would be the point of that? That's not "giving it all." That's just giving up. If you're gonna do something, be there and get all you can from it. Don't sit and complain the whole time. Just do what you came to do.

Every day offers us another chance to give it all. When you're at work and you have a choice between doing something just well enough to get by or making it the best it can be, which do you choose? A lot of people don't like their jobs. I get that, but it's no excuse to settle for being lazy, because the kind of results you deliver will become your trademark. If you need a plumber, and you ask your friends for recommendations, are you going to hire the one who everybody says did an "okay" job or the one who people say put out the extra effort to make his work perfect? I know which plumber I would call to work in my house.

Being a good friend operates on the same principle. We all know people who are fun to hang out with but aren't reliable when we need a helping hand. Which kind of pal do you want to be? More important, which sort of friend do you want *your* friends to know you are? Make the extra effort to be good to your friends, and not just the ones closest to you. Is one of your coworkers moving? Get your work gloves and grab the end of the sofa instead of carrying that one flimsy lamp. Does your neighbor feel overwhelmed because she's caring for a new baby? Offer to watch the kid for a while so she can run errands, or even just enjoy a long shower in peace. Have you heard through the grapevine that someone you know is having money troubles? Think about sliding them an interest-free loan instead of buying yourself some expensive thing you don't really need. Offer someone a ride, even if it means going out of your way. Give a hungry person half your sandwich.

Maybe you don't want to embarrass your friends or family members by offering them help they haven't asked for. Okay, but have you considered that maybe they feel embarrassed to ask for assistance? Sometimes, all it takes to make the world a slightly better place is for one person to stop feeling self-conscious and just start doing the right thing. It might feel weird at first, but you'll get over it, and the more you do it, the easier it will be to do things without ever having to wonder, *What's in this for me?*

There might even come a day when someone—maybe a member of your family, or maybe a stranger—asks you for something really serious, like a donation of bone marrow or one of your kidneys. This is life-or-death stuff. Forget all the stories you hear about soldiers risking their lives for one another in combat; this kind of moment is when you find out who the real heroes are. When you have a comfortable, safe life and choose to make a sacrifice like this, that's what "giving it all" is really about: putting other people ahead of yourself.

Another important aspect of "give it all" is this: don't go cheap on yourself or your loved ones. I'm not saying you should go broke, but do the most you can and don't cut corners on things that matter. Some things in life you can buy at a discount without worrying—paper clips, for instance, or paper towels, and maybe toothpicks.

As a general rule, when it comes to anything that you count on to protect your health, safety, or life, I recommend you spend just a little bit extra. To use a snowboarding example, if you're ready to take the plunge, don't buy cheap safety equipment or a shoddy board. That's not a time or place for going half-assed—that's a situation where you want to spend what it takes to get gear you can trust. If you don't, the only one you're hurting is yourself.

If you're already spending thousands of dollars on a new car, spring for passenger-side air bags and antilock brakes. When you buy a house, spend a few hundred dollars to put in proper smoke alarms and carbon-monoxide detectors. If you bring a baby into this world, you have a duty as a parent to get life insurance and buy the best infant car seats you can.

That's just my opinion, of course. But I'm pretty sure I'm right.

There are other times when it's good to go all in for yourself. I know it's important to save money for the big things in life—buying a home or a car, sending a child to college, or just having cash on hand in case of an emergency—but if you become a fanatic about it, pretty soon all you think about is the money in your bank account, and you stop thinking about why you're acquiring it.

If there's something you think you really need, or something that you desperately want, maybe you should just get it. I'm not saying spend as if you're the only one who knows the world is ending the day before your credit-card bill will show up, but if there's something important that you want to buy, and you keep coming back to thinking about how much better, or easier, or more productive your life would be if only you had it . . . well, that might be a sign that you should stop making excuses and look for a way to make the purchase. Maybe this'll mean taking out a bank loan (if you can afford the payments!), or getting a part-time job, but that's all right. You're worth it.

This becomes even more important when you're looking to do something grand for someone else. I know a guy who thought about dropping out of an expensive college after his first year because he thought his parents couldn't afford the tuition. His father told him to go back to school and not worry about it. When registration day came, a check for the full cost of the semester arrived, as if out of nowhere. Months later, my friend went home for Thanksgiving— and realized only then that his dad had sold his car and taken a part-time second job to make sure his son had the chance to finish his education and follow his dream.

That is what I mean by "give it all."

But it's not just about money. In fact, sometimes just giving money is a bit of a cop-out and *not* giving it your all. If there is a cause you feel really passionate about—well, yes, it's nice to make a financial contribution. But you make a much greater impact if you give your time. Giving *yourself* is huge.

It's the same thing with friendship. You can be a fun friend, hang out, enjoy good times, but true friendship means becoming invested in another person's life. It means you're there for good times and bad. It means really listening, hearing what the other person is saying, and really caring. It means sometimes thinking of the other person first instead of just thinking of yourself. Yeah, it means giving it your all.

This philosophy of total commitment is what kept me pushing my limits in rehab at Walter Reed. I never wanted to settle for minimum standards, or for "good enough," or for "almost." I wanted to be the best person I could be. That meant putting everything I had into getting myself back to good, no matter how many times I had to fall to get there. If you're wondering whether you're giving it all, I guess a good rule of thumb would be: "Are you falling yet?"

Sure, I could have pushed myself less and still gotten through the basic steps of my rehab. There was always someone around who was happy to tell me to "take it easy" and advise me not to tire myself out. I'm sure those folks all meant well, but what would listening to them have gained me? Nothing, that's what. If I had given in to temptation and taken the easy way, my rehab would only have taken longer and I would have gotten less out of it. That's not doing myself a favor; that's ripping myself off.

There will always be people around you who are willing to let you off the hook. Don't let them. I'm not saying push yourself too far; I don't want you to hurt yourself. Just don't settle for less than your best effort. Don't quit until you know you've given everything you have. Be able to look anyone in the eye when you're done and be able to say, "I gave it all."

The same thing applies to my work with Quantum Rehab. I have a lot of creative input regarding the photos I appear in. When you see me on a poster or in a magazine ad, you can be sure I wasn't just some mannequin that got posed in front of a camera. I care about the messages I help promote. I ask to see a sketch of the project; I want to know what the slogan will be. In a lot of cases, I think up those ads myself because I have something I want to say, an image I want to project to the world. I'm not gonna churn something out just to fill space, or to show off something I did. Anytime my face is on something, I want to be proud of that, I want to be happy I made that choice—and I want everyone who sees those images to know that I stand behind them, that I believe in the ideas they express.

If you don't give it all, no matter what it is you do or make, if you let yourself get away with doing something half-assed, you're not going to be proud of it. You're not going to look at it as an accomplishment. You'll just be filling the world with more mediocre crap. Don't we already have more of that than we could possibly use? Never settle for producing something that's just "good enough." Dig deep and create something that'll make people say, "Damn! That's cool!"

Another big part of giving it all is not being afraid to fail. Failure is not always a bad thing. There is no shame in coming up short of your goal as long as you maintain a good attitude. If you give it all in everything that you do, even when things don't work out the way you hope, you won't have any reason to feel ashamed. In those circumstances, you can tell yourself, *I did all I could. I gave my best, I made every effort.* As long as your heart is in what you do, you're never going to feel like you've wasted your time.

You are what you do, which is why you should always do your best, even when you feel your worst. In fact, when you feel your worst is when it's most important to fight to be your best.

If you chase a dream and fail, odds are you'll learn something along the way, or perhaps at least have fun in the attempt. That's why I say that I don't regret anything, because everything I've done has given me something valuable: experience or a pleasant memory—or if I'm lucky, both. My failures have given me skills and knowledge that helped me later in life when I was doing something else. That's why I don't let setbacks get me down: I know that someday the insight I've just gained might be just what I need to help me pick myself back up.

Perhaps the most important reason for giving it all is the one that's the least selfish. Forget about what *you* gain by giving your best and think about what it means to other people. In a lot of ways, life is like millions of parallel lines of dominoes, and which ones fall depends on one decision at the start of a long chain of events. As much as we need to choose to give our best, what our best might be at any moment depends on a lot of things beyond our control: the resources available to us, the place in which we find ourselves, and whether there are trained people ready to help us. Sometimes, by giving our all we make it possible for someone else to do the same. In other words, we owe it to one another to be our best selves. We need one another.

My mom has always understood this idea. The work she did and the sacrifices she made for me while I was at Walter Reed made it possible for me to give everything I had to my rehab process. I was able to focus all my strength on getting my life back because she always made sure the day-to-day stuff—the paperwork, the cooking, the cleaning, and more paperwork—got done. So when I talk about how I "gave it all" in rehab to put myself back together, it's vital to remember that the only reason I was able to do it was that my mom was giving *her* all to make sure that I could. But she didn't stop there. My mom saw the bigger picture.

When she wasn't doing stuff to help me, she was finding ways to help other people—other wounded vets and their families. She made friends with all the other soldiers' mothers at Walter Reed, and then she teamed up with a woman named Maria, the mother of another wounded soldier, to start a program to help the families of new patients at the hospital acclimate to their situations.

When my folks first arrived in Washington, D.C., no one was there to explain things to them. When they first got off the plane, they didn't know where to go. No one met them at the airport. They had to find their own way to Walter Reed. Then they walked into the hospital, looked around, and my mom and dad asked each other, "Now what?"

That was more hassle and stress than they should have had to put up with at a time like that. My mom understood this. But it's not this that makes her special. What makes her special is that she *did* something about it.

She and Maria and some other mothers created a program in which family members who have been at Walter Reed for a while go to the airports or train stations and meet the arriving family members of incoming patients. They escort the new folks to Walter Reed, show them around, explain how things work, and tell them who to talk to in order to get things done. It's a way for people who have already had time to adjust to make the process easier for families that are just starting such a confusing journey during a traumatic period in their lives.

My mom was an active part of the program while we were at Walter Reed, but now that we've left, it continues on its own, with new people arriving, becoming part of it, and then paying it forward to the next wave of families in need. The reason it exists, though, is because my mom rallied a few other people and helped get that ball rolling. She and her friends, despite being in the midst of their own very painful ordeals, gave their best so that others could do the same. Watching my mom in action was one of the greatest things I have ever seen, and it made me want to live my life the same way.

Honestly, I think this is the only way to live. Demand the best from yourself. Give your best in everything you do and to everyone you meet. Create the best work that you can, and try to create situations that help and encourage other people to be and do their best. Imagine for a minute what kind of world this would be if everyone did this even half the time. Picture a life in which everyone you meet pushes themselves and refuses to settle for half-assed crap. Think about how much cleaner our streets would be, how much healthier we'd be, how much better everything would work. That would be a world to be proud of, a life worth working your ass off to preserve. Does this sound crazy? Does it seem impossible?

Well, it isn't. The only thing keeping us from living in that world is ourselves and the people around us. All it takes to get there is for each of us to start by improving ourselves, becoming our best, and doing what we can to lead others down the same road. It won't happen overnight, but if we don't get to work, it will never happen.

So go out and start giving life your all.

6

CHANGE CAN BE GOOD

I once heard that the secret to not dying is to never do anything for the last time. That's a nice idea, but I think I have a better one: the secret to *really living* is to always try to be doing something for the *first* time.

This is how my brother, Bobby, and I approached everything when we were kids. We were athletes, and playing one sport was never enough to keep us interested. As soon as we got good at one, we wanted to learn another. By the time we finished junior high school, we had played baseball, football, and basketball. After we started high school, we set our sights on a new challenge: gymnastics. It looked hard but also fun, and we just knew we had to try it.

It turns out we were naturals—at least, that's what our coaches told us. Soon we were completely focused on gymnastics, and because we're twin brothers, we couldn't help but get really competitive with each other. Even though gymnastics can be a team sport, in a lot of ways it's really about individual performance, and that's what Bobby and I focused on. If you had asked him at any point during high school whether he was worried about beating the other schools in competition, he'd have told you, "I don't care about beating any of them. The only person that I care about beating is my brother." To be honest, I'd have said the same thing.

When we practiced, if one of us did a cool new move, the other would say, "That's awesome, bro!" Then we'd think, *Now I need to come up with something to one-up him.*

Learning gymnastics made for some of the best times my brother and I have ever had together, and we owed it all to the fact that we were willing to try something new just for the sake of the experience. Changing our sport made us better athletes and stronger competitors.

After high school, when an injury put an end to my dream of becoming an Olympic gymnast, Bobby and I both got jobs at American Airlines as members of the ground crew at O'Hare International Airport. Working together was fun at first. Starting a new job is always an interesting time. You're learning new things and meeting new people. Soon, though, you settle in. Then comes the routine.

That was part of why I joined the Army.

You see, every evening Bobby and I were hanging out with the same friends, in the same pool hall, night in and night out, for about a year and a half. There was never any variety—never a trip to Six Flags, or to a Cubs game, or an afternoon on the beach. Just the same old routine.

One day my brother said, "I need a change. It's time for me to get out of here."

"What do you mean by that?"

"I put in for a transfer to Texas."

I didn't think anything of it at the time. After all, just because he had asked for a transfer didn't mean he would ever get it. I assumed he was just blowing off steam, and I forgot about it.

Two weeks later, he waved a piece of paper in my face. "Hey, I got that transfer. I'm outta here. Later." The next thing I knew, Bobby was gone, and I'd been left behind. I had no idea what to do. I knew I wasn't satisfied with the life I had, but I felt stuck, so I just kept on doing the same boring shit for another year and a half.

Don't get me wrong. I liked the work I did at American Airlines. I loved the people I worked with, and I enjoyed hanging out with my friends. None of the individual parts of my life made me unhappy—it was the fact that I couldn't see anything more to my life beyond my daily grind. Eventually, I reached a point where I knew exactly what my whole month was going to be like because nothing ever changed, and I realized it was never going to change unless *I* changed it. Like my brother, I needed something different. Life was *out there*, and I was missing it.

That's why, in April 2001, my girlfriend, Lisa, and I went down to the military recruiters' office. We talked to reps from the Marine Corps, the Air Force, the Navy, and the Army. We figured out fairly quickly that the Army would be the best fit for us. Since I don't want to risk ticking off too many of my fellow veterans, I'll keep my reasons to myself.

I said to the Army recruiter, "I think I'd like to be a military police officer. I've always wanted to know if I could be a cop and see if that's what I want to do with my life."

"Your test scores are high enough," he said. "You could be a police officer if you want. We'll send you in." He pulled out a stack of paperwork for me to fill out in triplicate.

Then Lisa asked him the million-dollar question: "Is there any way we can do this together? Go to the same basic training, the same duty stations, and all that?"

The recruiter looked at her and then at me, and he raised one eyebrow suspiciously. "Not really. This is the Army, not the Holiday Inn."

"Really?" I said. "Are you sure there's absolutely *no way* we can do this together?"

"Short of being married, no, there isn't."

I don't know if he heard the gears turning inside my head or smelled the smoke from the thought taking shape inside Lisa's, but he must have known what we were thinking, because he started shaking his head. "No, no, no. Let's not do anything drastic, okay?"

We promised him we wouldn't.

On the drive home, I looked at Lisa. "Hey, wanna get married?"

Lisa said yes, so what happened next wasn't *entirely* my fault.

We went to the courthouse. I paid ten dollars for a marriage license, and we got married.

We went back to the recruitment office. Boy, was the Army recruiter *thrilled* to see us again. He wrote up our orders, which arranged for us to be sent to the same basic-training facility and eventually deployed to the same duty station. We signed up for the "delayed entry" program so that we would have time to settle our civilian affairs, put our stuff into storage, and all that other mundane bullshit, before we had to report for basic training in September.

Most people would have used those five months to prepare themselves mentally, physically, and emotionally for what they were about to do to their lives. Lisa and I didn't. We spent roughly a month partying like animals, and at the end of it we made a profound discovery: We didn't want to be married anymore. Lisa suggested we file for divorce, and I agreed.

She filled out the paperwork and paid the fee. It cost nine hundred dollars, which made no sense to me. Why did it cost only ten bucks to get married but nine bills to get divorced? Years later, one of my Army buddies explained it to me: the reason divorce is so expensive is because it's worth it.

So getting married was a good change that turned bad. Getting divorced seemed like a bad change that turned out to be one of the best decisions I've ever made.

When it comes to making changes in your life, things aren't always what they seem.

I didn't realize how much of the world I had been missing out on until I got blown up in Iraq. After I was discharged from rehab, I started realizing, *Wow—there's so much out there!* Some people might think it's ironic that now that I was seemingly less mobile I was realizing how big the world is. Actually, I've traveled more in the last few years than in my entire life before I was blown-up. These days, I just want to go to new places all the time. If there were any blank spaces left on the map of the world, I'd be on my way there with my camera in my hand.

Now, I'm all about experiencing everything at least once. I've done some things people might think are crazy. I've had my nipples pierced, I've had my eyebrow pierced, I got my tongue pierced, and I have multiple tattoos. I'll do just about anything that seems like it might be fun, just to *do it*. I'll taste a food I've never eaten, or jump off a bungee tower. Whatever it is, I'm down with it. I want to do everything at least once, or at least try to do it. I want to experience everything I possibly can in my short-ass life. No matter what it is or how it works out, it means I always have something new to think about, talk about, or look forward to. It's the best way I know to keep life from getting boring.

This is part of why I don't like hearing other people sell me short. Not doctors, not friends, no one. Never tell me what I *can't* do, because I'll prove you wrong every time. For instance, I can still climb a tree. And you wouldn't think I'd be able to learn how to drive a quad all-terrain vehicle with no legs and one hand, but I knew I could do it. Sure, I needed help from my friends at work to modify the quad with special hand controls and hip braces to keep me in the seat, but I always knew it *could be done*. Anything can be done if you have the will to do it.

I think one of the most important parts of living a full life is to seek out what's new. Go to new places. Meet new people. Do new things. Eat new foods, consider new ideas, listen to new music, learn a new language—whatever it is that excites you. If it's new and you think it might be fun, try it. What have you got to lose? Whatever it might cost you in cash or time, it'll probably be worth it. Money gets spent, stuff can be destroyed, but your memories are yours. An interesting life is something no one can ever take away from you.

Of course, I'm not saying to go totally bat-shit crazy. Don't do something that causes harm to yourself or others or puts anyone—yourself included—in danger. It should go without saying that anything illegal, immoral, or just stupid and reckless should be off-limits. You have to stay alive to have an interesting life, so use some common sense while pushing your boundaries.

Be smart, but don't be afraid. I'm just saying you should expose yourself to new things, make your life an adventure. You also have to be willing to put yourself out there in other ways. Take some chances on yourself—trust your instincts. Case in point: I had a great idea for a new kind of wheelchair. I wanted a wheelchair that could dance—a computer program that would move the chair automatically so you could have both hands on your partner instead of having to use a joystick to make the chair move. Maybe it was kind of "out there," but I was sure I was onto something. When I have an idea like that, I don't hide it away. Even if it doesn't work out, so what? If someone doesn't like it, or they think it's crazy, we can still have a good laugh about it. But if someone else sees in it what I see in it, then maybe we've got something, y'know? So I pitched my wheelchair idea to a friend in the research-and-development division at Quantum Rehab. He thought it sounded like a cool idea, and he asked me to submit it as a formal proposal.

Well, I'd never written a proposal before. I don't know what one looks like. I wouldn't even know where to start. But I was determined to do it because it's something I'd never done before, and I wanted to learn how. So I talked to a couple of people, found out what I had to do, and submitted my idea. And who knows? If it works out, I might help create something totally new, something no one's ever thought of before. It would be worth getting laughed at for a *hundred* times, just to have that feeling of success *once*.

Every time in my life when I felt as if the whole world was crashing down on my shoulders, when I felt like I couldn't breathe and nothing was ever gonna work out again, when I was in the darkest, shittiest mood you could imagine, somehow things have always turned out for the better. Setbacks and disappointments suck, but somehow they open my eyes to better ideas, to possibilities I wouldn't have even considered if everything had gone smoothly.

A lot of us don't realize that just because something bad happens, it doesn't mean everything is gonna be bad forever. It could turn out to be the best thing that's ever happened to your life. For the most part, all the things in life that I thought were horrid, or the worst thing ever, turned out to be the best thing ever. I mean, I'm not gonna say that getting my legs blown off was the best thing that could've happened to me, but that experience has given me so many opportunities that I can't see it as a bad thing. It forced me to grow and see life with new eyes; it created job opportunities I would never have pursued; it made me a public figure and gave me a chance to stand up in front of congressmen and be heard on behalf of other people. I doubt I could have done that if I was just another guy who came home from Iraq without a scratch.

Once you recognize that things that seem terrible might prove to be wonderful, you can live with no limits. You can go where you want to go, fly as high as you want, and do what you want to do—and nothing that anyone else says can ever hold you down again.

Sometimes I hear people say, "I'm thinking about moving to this place or that place, but I don't want to start all over. I don't have any friends there. I don't have enough money." It's been my experience that when you get put into a situation where you're uncomfortable, you don't know anyone, and you don't know the details, that's when you'll learn a lot about yourself. You'll meet so many different people and gain tons of new opportunities, most of which you would never have expected. You'll *learn*. That experience is great. It's how you grow.

So one of my philosophies—and it doubles as one of my most frequent bits of advice—is that I think everyone should move away from whatever place they think of as "home" for at least a year. In that time, as you meet new people, you learn (or relearn) how to make new friends, take care of yourself, and find your way around a new place. You have no idea how many new opportunities can come from something like that.

I'm not saying abandon everything familiar forever. You don't need to turn your back permanently on a place you like and people you love. I'm just saying have the courage to try something new and test your limits. Find out what you're really capable of becoming.

A perfect time to try something like this is when you feel as if you've lost everything. When you've run out of options, and everything seems hopeless, moving to a strange place might seem like the last thing you'd want to do. But that's exactly the moment when you're most free. That's your chance to let go of a life that doesn't work and go make a new one that does.

I've gotten to a point where I like changing my setting every couple of years. I like getting a fresh take and starting over. It's what I did when I joined the Army: I just threw myself into that, even though I had no idea what was going on, where I would be sent, or what I would be doing once I got there. Once I was in, I adapted and found my way, one day at a time. The knowledge I gained from that experience was priceless.

Then, when I woke up in Walter Reed, I thought, *Well, I guess I'll move home*. I mean, sure, I had friends and family back in Rolling Meadows, but a lot of them had moved on, and I felt as if I didn't really know anyone there—but I didn't let that stop me. I went back and lived with my parents for a while. Before long, I knew I wanted my own place. I had no idea whether I'd be able to manage living alone, but I was ready to give it a try. So I left, made my own way, and learned how to live by myself in a regular apartment, just like everyone else does.

When I first started working for Quantum Rehab, I spent a lot of time at its headquarters in northeastern Pennsylvania. One of the first people I met was Henry, a stick-thin dude with spiky hair and some cool tattoos. He said to me one day, "Y'know, there's this girl who works here who has blond hair with hot-pink highlights." This came up because I used to love to dye my hair all kinds of colors. I was like a walking rainbow for a while. I've had green hair, red hair, blue hair, you name it. All the guys at Quantum loved it. They still ask me to dye my hair once in a while, but I'm kind of over it. To me, changing my hair color was about expressing myself and getting people to realize you can't judge a person based on something as superficial as that. Just because I look a certain way, it doesn't tell you anything about who I am. That was my whole reason for dyeing my hair. The fact that the top of my head looked like a parakeet didn't mean that I didn't know what I was doing or that I wasn't serious or professional about my work.

Anyway, Henry told me, "You've gotta meet this girl, Kaleena."

"All right," I said. When I got into the office the next morning, I said to Henry, "Take me to this girl." He walked me over to her desk. When I met her, she and I instantly clicked. We just under-

90

stood each other right off the bat, and pretty soon we became best friends. She kind of adopted me and began opening up my social circle. I met her family and her friends. Her boyfriend rides quads, and he invited me to come out one Sunday and go riding with him on the back of his quad. Excited at the idea, I said, "Sure! Let's do it."

That Sunday we went riding up on the mountain, and we had a great time. After that, I said to one of my new friends, "I think I want to buy a quad." I bought a quad and started going out on Sundays, riding the trails with all these people I had just met.

That's how it happens: it snowballs. By meeting one new person, you meet three. Each of them brings three more into the picture. Before long, I was a part of this place, and it was a part of me. Just like that, because I was open to the possibilities in front of me, I had a new home.

Not being shy is another thing I've learned. I used to let people walk all over me when I was younger. To be frank, I was kind of a pushover. I give the Army a lot of the credit for helping me change that. My training taught me to be direct in my actions and to know that what I'm doing is right. Confidence can't be taught but it can be nurtured. It's a quality you can develop if you're given the chance, and if you give yourself the chance. You acquire it through your experiences, by watching people and learning. It's almost as if it's the sum of everything else you do, an equation you solve simply by living with your eyes open.

I became truly confident when I stopped second-guessing myself. It's good sometimes to ask questions, but if you're always questioning your choices, you'll never be sure of what you want, what you believe in, or what to do. I've learned to trust my instincts, and that makes me self-assured. It's the key to everything else that I do.

Confidence is probably the single-most attractive quality in the world. It makes other people feel at ease, because they sense your faith in yourself, and they figure that if you believe in yourself, then they can believe in you, too. People like having something or someone to believe in. Understanding that simple human truth has opened a lot of doors for me.

Confidence is vital to many parts of life, but it's never more important than when you're trying to get a date. This was especially true after I got blown up. I wasn't sure how to approach a girl. Would she ever see me as more than a guy in a wheelchair who could be a friend? Could she find me sexually attractive?

I was on my first trip for Pride Mobility and I was at one of our dealers' stores. I was talking to a group of employees and I invited them all out to dinner. Well, there was this one girl who was really nice and cute, and I was talking to her most of the night. At the end of the dinner, I asked if she wanted to come back to my room to listen to some music. She did, and we actually dated for a while after that.

I have a lot more confidence with girls these days because I have a lot more confidence in myself. I know now that women can see me as a sexual man. And I'll let you in on a little secret: sex actually got better after I got blown up. I'm not kidding. Sex with no legs is great. This might not seem like the kind of change that I would be calling "good," but it really is. There are so many positions I can get into now that I couldn't when my legs were in the way. The geometry is completely different and so is my center of balance, but it's amazing how much more stamina I have now that my body weighs so much less. Maybe I'm not every gal's dream lover, but I haven't heard anyone complain yet.

Embracing change is all about being willing to learn about yourself. When you're afraid of change, that's fear talking. That's your doubt. That's your subconscious trying to hold you back because you don't want to cope with failure, or disappointment, or rejection, or loneliness. But you have to push past that. Diving headfirst into change is about improving yourself, even if it hurts. *Especially* if it hurts. Uprooting your life, or quitting your job, or ditching a botched relationship might seem like the scariest thing in the world, but it's probably the greatest gift you can ever give to yourself.

Just to confuse you, sometimes change is *not* good. Changes that are designed to baby you or remove challenges that might help you grow are not what you should want. Push those sorts of changes away. If you find yourself facing two choices, and one seems really hard while the other seems really easy, it's usually a good bet that the hard way is the right way.

For example, when I bought my condo in Rolling Meadows, my family and friends started talking about "adapting" the place to my "needs." They were talking about lowering the countertops and cabinets, putting in special fixtures in the bathroom, that kind of shit. I said to them, "No, you're gonna build this place the way you would for anyone else." I didn't want special treatment. I didn't want anyone trying to make things easy for me. I wanted everything in my home to be normal. By keeping things that way, I'm not coddled. I'm not catered to.

Thanks to that decision, when I'm out in the real world, I don't find myself paralyzed by unfamiliar situations: "Uh-oh—there's no curb cut here! What do I do?" I already know what to do and how to do it. I face basic challenges in my everyday life so that they will *be* familiar to me when I'm in public. So now I can go anywhere I want, whether it's handicapped accessible or not. Once I got used to always doing things the hard way, it stopped seeming so hard.

I'm not saying that there aren't people who don't need the lowered cabinets and curb cuts. People who genuinely need those things should have them and use them and not feel any less proud of who they are. I'm just saying that people who don't *need* those bits of extra help ought to learn to do without them. If you can get by without small, coddling luxuries, it will only make you stronger and better prepared to experience more of the real world. You'll work harder, but the reward is something you can't put a price tag on: *freedom.*

I don't understand why, but too many people I've met who are in wheelchairs but otherwise still fit (i.e., not completely paralyzed) rarely or never go out into the real world. There are a few people who I see outside all the time, pushing their limits, but for each one of them I know that there are tons of other folks in wheelchairs who don't even leave their houses.

I know it's partly because insurance companies won't pay for any kind of mobility device that lets people go outside, because they apparently don't believe disabled people need to go outside, and that's an attitude we need to correct. In a large number of cases, however, it's simply because those people are afraid, or because they've given up on their life. They dwell on what has happened to them instead of seeing how much they still have left to do.

Basically, they're just rolling over and dying instead of choosing to get up and fight, and that's not living—that's just existing. *Existing* isn't enough. We need to *live*, damn it!

I'll leave you with this thought, and you can make of it what you will. Change can be painful, inconvenient, expensive, and upsetting. It might lead to good things, or it might not. A lot of us try to avoid change whenever we can. We like things the way they are, and we'd prefer that life not come along and mess up all our pretty things once we finally get them the way we want them. Well, too bad. Changes aren't permanent, but change is, so you need to learn how to cope with it and make it your friend instead of your enemy. There is only one time when you can count on nothing in your life changing for you ever again, and that will be when you're dead.

Embrace change no matter what form it takes—because it means you're *still alive*.

7

THERE IS NO BOX

Memo to the world at large: stop telling me to "think outside the box." What pisses me off about it is the assumption that I live or think inside a box in the first place. I don't see the world that way, and I don't think you should either. However, I ought to confess that over the past few years, I've told countless people to think outside the box, and in all likelihood I'll use the phrase again many more times. It's one of those shorthand expressions that people kind of get right away, but that doesn't make it any less trite. If ever you hear me say that phrase again, remind me of this simple truth: *there is no box.*

The box is different for each person and situation, but in general it means anything that limits your perception, restrains your possibilities, or inhibits your actions. It might be a narrow set of assumptions about the way something works or what you are allowed to do. For some people, the box is a mental or physical handicap; for others, it's a lack of money, education, courage, or any of a hundred other things without which they think they can't succeed or be happy. It might be a set of rules, or a religious code, a dead-end job, or plain old fear. And they let these perceived limitations restrict what they can achieve. Some people realize what's going on and resent it, like someone who becomes a lawyer or gets married because that's what their parents want them to do. Others don't even realize they're in a box and seem perfectly happy within whatever limits they've accepted, like "Why would I want to do that? Men (or women) don't do that." Or "That's not what we do where I come from." It's a shame. But the truth is that none of those things matter unless you think they do.

So, if boxes are bad, why do we let ourselves get shoved inside them? I think it starts when we're kids, and the adults in our lives need to control us. They slap labels on us, call us good kids or bad kids, smart or dumb, athletic or clumsy, and that makes their lives easier. Maybe we let them because we're hardwired to want to know where we stand in the pecking order, but I think it's probably just because we all start out scared or confused or just hungry for approval. So we go along to get along, to avoid punishment or maybe just to fit in.

As we get older, the pattern continues. The world builds up one box after another around us, adding more labels and limitations to our lives until we're nested inside so many of these shells that breaking free starts to seem harder than trying to escape from Alcatraz. Impossible though it might first appear, escaping from these invisible prisons is what we all need to do. We aren't meant to live like this.

No one can put you into a box unless you let them. The only boxes that define the boundaries of your life are the ones you put yourself into, or that you permit other people to put you into. In a sense, each of us becomes our own jailer. What most of us don't realize, however, is that we also hold the keys that will set us free. All it takes to be free is to see that the box isn't real.

Most of this stuff is just custom. Some people take these ideas for granted and swear by them, but they can really be kind of random if you think about it. I mean, men used to wear wigs all the time. How did that happen? Now we make fun of guys who wear toupees. Customs change. They can change so much because there's nothing real about them. Wear a wig, don't wear a wig. What difference does it make?

There is no box.

Usually, this topic comes up when people ask me how I get through my daily life despite the injuries I suffered in Iraq. They see that I have no legs, and they ask me how I get around. "What if," they ask, "you go someplace with stairs and no elevators? Then what do you do?" Some of them look at my prosthetic hand and ask me how I handle a fork and knife or get dressed by myself. When I tell them that I can drive a car, even one that hasn't been modified with special hands-only controls, just a regular car, the same as theirs, they can't believe it. I might as well tell them I've just cured cancer—I'd be met by the same blank, stupid stare.

What's happening in those situations is that some people, when they first meet me, don't really see *me*. What they see is the box that they assume I live in, the limitations they imagine must define and confine my life. Instead of a man, they see a set of injuries and a wheelchair and a paint-by-numbers war story. Other folks I've met are more up front about their assumptions. They give my one-armed, legless body a once-over and say, "It must suck having to do things a certain way because of what happened to you."

I don't get mad at times like that. I see it as a chance to share my way of thinking with someone. "No," I say to them, "just because I do something *differently* than you do, that doesn't make it any *harder.* It's just a different way of doing it." Most of the time, they get it.

Forgetting about the box is about learning to think bigger and see the possibilities in everything around you. Let me give you an example. Washing dishes was kind of tough for me. I have standard-height counters in my kitchen, and when I'd roll up to the sink in my wheelchair, I'd have to reach up and stretch to wash the dishes. It was really uncomfortable. One day, I had the idea to just jump up on the counter and the sink was right there. It was so much easier. To me, that's (okay, I'm going to say it) thinking outside the box: being willing to believe that the traditional way of doing something might not be the best way or the only way.

To get to the next step—no box—you have to change your way of thinking.

Once I started changing my way of seeing the world around me, things began opening up. It was almost as if my horizon had expanded—my world got just a bit bigger each time. As new possibilities came into focus, I began to see that most of my so-called limitations were only in my head. The only thing holding me back was myself.

That was a breakthrough moment. As soon as I realized the box was just an illusion, it disappeared. I felt like a prisoner cutting myself free of my own chains. Instead of being locked inside a tiny set of assumptions about where I could go and what I could do in a wheelchair, I was standing on the edge of an endless frontier. I could go anywhere and do anything.

Nowadays, even though some folks still think of me as disabled, I'm often moving faster than the people around me. Whether I'm at work or out in bars or restaurants, I tend to leave my friends in the dust. I don't do it to be rude. Most of the time I can't help it. It's just a simple fact: on a straightaway, wheels are faster than feet. Nine times out of ten, I'm one of the fastest travelers in an airport. When I first started using a wheelchair, I didn't think that would be possible. I figured it would kind of suck to be in a wheelchair while scrambling through a crowd to make a connecting flight. And waiting for the elevator in an airport was such a pain in the ass, I figured out how to ride escalators in my chair. I've done this all over the country without any problem—except in Philadelphia. The last time I was there, it seemed the TSA agents were on the lookout for me. As soon as I cruised toward an escalator they practically threw their bodies in front of me: "No, no! *You* can't go on the escalator!"

I said, "Look, I know it says 'no strollers' and stuff, but do you really think I'd be going for the escalator if I couldn't do it?" I guess they were just worried about me, and I get that, but . . . guys, come on. I can do it. In reality, I move five times faster than your average passenger. So don't feel bad for me if you see me in an airport—I've got nothing to complain about. Except in Philly.

The point is, how you *perceive* your circumstances goes a long way toward determining whether they'll be a handicap or an advantage. Many people see a wheelchair as a limitation, but if you change your way of thinking, you can transform it into a more efficient mode of personal transportation than what you had before. Do it right and other people should envy you: "Hey, how come *that* guy gets to speed through here on wheels? Why can't *I* be in a wheelchair . . . ?"

Learning to live without boxes is about more than turning setbacks into opportunities. It's also about not letting other people take away your possibilities.

After I came home from Iraq, I learned not to listen to doctors when they told me all the things that I would never be able to do again. *Can't* is not in my vocabulary. I can *try.* If it doesn't work out, then it doesn't work out, but I can *always* try.

Don't listen to other people who want to tell you what your limits are. There's nothing stopping you in life except your own mind. When my doctors said to me, "We don't think you'll be able to do this," or "We don't think you should try to do that," it only made me want to do those things *more.* Being told that I *can't* do something just makes me want to push myself even harder. Maybe that's why doctors say it. Perhaps it's some kind of reverse psychology to goad patients into making the effort. Or not. I don't know. But when a doctor sees a patient who has been in a car wreck and suffered a spinal-cord injury, and they tell that person, "You'll never walk again," I don't think that's right. If they said that to me, I'd shoot back, "Screw you. Who are you to say that I'm never gonna walk again?" That's not their call to make, it's *mine.*

I'm not saying that positive thinking is going to repair a real spinal-cord injury. An optimistic outlook isn't magic. It won't raise the dead or bring back things that have been destroyed. Scars, whether physical or emotional, don't go away overnight. Sitting in your recliner and visualizing yourself winning a million dollars won't make it happen—believe me, I speak from experience. Long, bitterly disappointing experience.

What I'm talking about is taking charge of your own mind. Everything else depends on that first step. Changing your point of view is what makes it possible to see options that you might have missed. It's an essential part of building your self-confidence so that you can be the one who tells other people who you are and what you can do.

No matter what you do, people will still try to fit you into boxes. It might seem as if the easiest thing to do is to let it happen; after all, it doesn't matter as long as you know the box is an illusion, right? Wrong. If you don't stand up for yourself and refuse to be boxed, how will other people know the way you feel? Part of being free of the box is not letting others put you back inside one. Show others what it means to not be a number or a label but a free human being.

One thing to look out for is when well-meaning people—be they family, friends, colleagues, or strangers—try to disguise the box as a pedestal. It might feel like you're being propped up and lavished with praise, fame, and glory, but this is when you need to be on your guard: you're just being fitted for a different, prettier kind of box.

Sometimes, both happen at the same time.

After I came home from Iraq, different groups and individuals wanted to hold me up as a symbol for whatever agenda they were pushing. Some wanted to paint me as a hero, and others wanted the world to see me as a victim. What they all were missing is that

I just wanted to be seen as myself—as Bryan Anderson, a fun-loving guy from Illinois.

As far as my experience in Iraq is concerned, I don't see what happened to me on my last afternoon in Baghdad as a tragedy. You might see it that way, but I don't, and that difference matters. Calling it a tragedy makes me a victim. A victim has no control. Victims are treated like spectators to their own lives. Describing my combat experience as tragic and shoving me into a box labeled "victim" diminishes me, and it robs my military service of its honor and dignity. I served by choice, and I don't regret any of my experiences, not even the one that cost me three limbs. I'm a soldier, and I was proud to serve and make my sacrifice. I will *never* let someone slap a label on me and take all that away. To me, that day was just another life experience. I've learned from it, gained great new opportunities from it, embraced it, and made it part of who I am.

On the flip side, though, some people have told me that I'm a hero. I don't know about that. I was just a guy driving a Humvee that got blown up. My wounds were extreme, but my story is far too common. There are literally thousands of other veterans who were wounded as I was, and more getting hit every day as I write this. If I'm a hero, so are they . . . and I'm okay with that, I guess. But I think a lot of them would tell you the same thing I'm about to: We're just soldiers, and this is our job. We won't ask for your pity, but we deserve your respect.

The bottom line here is that I don't have to accept a label, either positive or negative, just because it would make it easier for someone else to define me. I don't have to see myself that way. I am who I *choose* to be.

When people talk about me, I don't want them to say, "Bryan

Anderson? Oh, yeah, he's that guy who got fucked up in the war."
I don't want people to think of me in terms of what *happened* to
me: I want them to notice how I *live* and what I *do*. I am more than
a wounded veteran. I'm an athlete: a snowboarder, a quad driver,
and a skateboarder. I'm a national spokesperson for Quantum
Rehab. I'm an actor and activist. I'm a man.

One moment will not define me or my life. I am what I do.

This is your chance to make the same declaration. What boxes
have you been living in? Are you defining yourself by a job you
hate, a relationship that has run its course, or something that happened to you against your will? Look at yourself in the mirror and
set yourself free. Say to your reflection, "I am not my dumb job. I
am not my shitty relationship. I am not a victim."

You need to *believe* what you're saying. Get angry about it if
that's what it takes. All our lives people punish us for getting angry.
Our parents and teachers and bosses tell us to calm down. Friends
and strangers get nervous when we show strong emotions. Screw
them. When we've been wronged, mistreated, lied to, or taken
advantage of, getting mad is *exactly* the right reaction. There's no
shame in it. On the road to self-change, a deep reserve of righteous
anger can be a gift. Use it if that's what it takes to free yourself
from a prison made of labels.

Once you figure out what you're not, you need to be ready to
answer bigger questions: Who are you? How do you define yourself?
What do you want people to notice about you? It's easy to tell yourself, *I am not a victim*, but if you keep referring to yourself that way
when you talk to other people, you're putting yourself back in the
box. You can't define yourself only by denying what others might
think, or what even you might have felt in the past. You have to

picture yourself in a positive way, not a negative way. Being free of the box is just the beginning of living a free life. The hard part is defining yourself through your actions and your attitude. Becoming the person you wish to be takes a lot of work and a lot of time. You'll have setbacks; there will be days when you'll feel like you're once again buried under boxes.

Break free, again and again, as many times as it takes. Don't settle for second best.

Find something you love and give it your all. Create something you can be proud of. Do something that makes the world a better place, or helps another person, or rights a wrong. Transform yourself from someone to whom things happen into a person who makes things happen. Step out of the shadows and take center stage in your own life.

Enriching your life with new experiences is the best way I know to help discover what really matters to you. Part of what helped me realize anything is possible is traveling, seeing new places, and meeting new people. It's amazing to me that no matter how many new places I visit, the people I've met always have a lot in common with one another. Even though it's a big world, in the ways that really matter, it's actually kind of small.

Some people are perfectly happy never seeing more than their own hometown. They have all they want right there, so they feel no need to travel.

Not me. Once I got a taste of the world, I knew I wanted more. I found out that I like learning about architecture, and I enjoy looking at art. I marvel at how much humanity has accomplished— in engineering, communications, and so much else—in such a short time. I've also confirmed through extensive firsthand research that

I don't like fish, not even the really expensive kinds, such as shrimp, lobster, or crab legs. I found out I'm also no fan of fishing. If I want to sit on a boat and drink beer, I'll go on a Caribbean cruise.

If I had listened to people who told me I was a handicapped victim who couldn't do this or that, I might never have left home. I'd still be in Rolling Meadows, Illinois, locked in a stupid little box, living down to someone else's pessimistic labels.

Screw that. I want to go everywhere, try everything, meet everyone, and see it all. I might not make it, but I'm on my way.

You can start your own journey right now. All it takes is a single instant of clarity, one moment when you can see past the labels and the lies and discover the truth for yourself:

There is no box.

Honestly, the way you think about yourself and your circumstances is *everything*. If you can change your way of thinking, you can change your life. You can change the world.

8

HOW WE SURVIVE

What is the first thing that you think of when you hear the word *survive*? When something awful happens to us, what does it really mean to survive the experience? To me, surviving means a whole lot more than simply not dying.

Emerging with a pulse on the other side of a shit storm is commendable, but if that's all you've got, it's not enough. That's just enduring punishment and continuing to *exist*. In my opinion, to really survive means accepting what has happened, picking yourself up, and going forward with the rest of your life, in whatever form it takes. The key word here is *life*. Existing is just taking up space and converting oxygen into carbon dioxide. Living is about growing and changing. Be honest with yourself: do you understand the difference?

I have to admit, before I got blown up in Iraq, I didn't really

109

see much of a distinction. Before that day in Baghdad, I saw things in black or white—you were either dead or alive. It wasn't until I got hit by an IED and ended up in rehab that I learned that there are shades of gray in everything, including life and death.

It can be hard to tell what'll happen to someone who suffers the kind of injuries I had. That kind of trauma can lead to infections; it can kill you in lots of different ways even after you get to the hospital. If you live through it, it can still end your life as you knew it. It can just blast away the hopes and dreams you had before it happened, and leave you with nothing.

I think that's what my family was most afraid of—that even after I recovered, I wouldn't be *me* anymore. That I'd be changed. Well, I was. Fortunately, I had been changed for the better.

One thing I had gained from my experience was a new sense of patience. I rolled out of the Walter Reed rehab clinic one afternoon, exhausted after a long, hard day of therapy. Sticking to my routine, I stopped outside the Malone House, where my mom and I shared a room, and I lit up a cigarette.

My mom joined me and asked, "How did therapy go?"

"It was shit," I said.

"Well, you need to remember that in time, this is all just gonna be a memory."

Hearing this immediately made everything better, because I knew she was right.

"Just keep pushing yourself," she said. "Do what you do, and it's going to be all right. You're going to get home in no time, and then you'll do whatever you want."

On bad days or on good days, my mom's message was always the same: "We're not gonna be here forever."

That was what I needed to hear, and she knew it. When I was deep in the grind of rehab, all I really wanted to do was go home. Mom's job was to remind me that the only road home ran through the rehab clinic. I started telling myself that Walter Reed was not the end of the line for me—it was just another stop on my way to freedom.

Remember the girl I told you about earlier in the book, the one who threatened to tear off her prosthetic legs if she fell? She was a bilateral who'd had two amputations, both below the knee. In other words, she still had both of her real knees, completely functional. She didn't seem to appreciate this at the time, but the fact that her knees were intact was a major advantage. The only thing that she really needed to get the hang of was balancing on her new limbs. Motion wasn't going to be a total grind for her the way it is for people who have lost one or both knees, as I did. But all she could focus on was the frustration of falling down.

She always had people do things for her that I think she should have done for herself. "Can you hand me my phone? . . . Can you get me a glass of water? . . . Can you push my chair?" As I said earlier, when she threatened to rip off her prosthetics if she fell again, it just pissed me off. I couldn't understand why someone with such a clear path to recovery would choose to give up. To me, her reaction seemed like a perfect example of the wrong way to tackle a problem. Her approach was a good way to grind to a halt and sink deeper down a hole. I wasn't gonna have that for myself. I knew my way would be more work, but since when did people start thinking of that as a bad thing?

The truth is, getting through rehab isn't easy for anybody. Before I started therapy, I was in a lot of pain. My arm hurt, my legs hurt, my stomach hurt. My whole body *hurt*. My doctors and therapists kept telling me, "You should get out of bed and into a wheelchair."

At the time I was in no mood to do the work that had to be done to get well. I was like "Guys, I just got blown up. Can't you just let me lie here awhile till I heal?" I didn't want to do anything. I just wanted to be left alone so I could rest. That's what I told myself, anyway. I think what was really happening was that I was in danger of just shutting down. If they had let me do that, I might have gotten used to being nothing more than a bump in a bed. If people had made daily life too easy for me, I might not have tried as hard to get my own life back.

Honestly, I didn't really get motivated until I saw my first set of prosthetics—and even then I had serious doubts. At that time I was the only bilateral, above-the-knee amputee in Walter Reed, so I didn't see anyone else with injuries like mine. Consequently, I wasn't sure I'd be able to handle the rehab regimen. The soldiers I saw were having enough trouble getting the hang of using one prosthetic limb, and I was looking at two C-legs and an arm. It was a lot to get my head around.

I couldn't help but wonder, *What happens if I'm not able to do this?* I knew I didn't want to be in a wheelchair the rest of my life. That was a lot of pressure at a time when I was already feeling really vulnerable. It didn't take long for all that anxiety piled on top of my pain and exhaustion to get me seriously down.

Luckily for me, my therapists made me get out of bed and do the work even when I didn't want to. I had good days and bad days; keeping myself on track was a struggle at first. During my stay at Walter Reed, I began suffering panic attacks. My heart would race, and I'd feel my pulse thudding in my head. At times I felt as if I was going to explode. Eventually I got so exhausted that I started to sink into a depression, and that's an emotional black hole that's really hard to get out of, even when you're surrounded by professionals who are trained to help you and by family members who throw you as many lifelines as it takes to pull you back into the light.

For some reason, as miserable as that experience was, it really helped put things into perspective for me. I realized that everybody gets hurt. We all have our problems. What makes us who we are is how we survive after bad things mess us up. It's what we do afterward that makes us who we are. So, when I finally started to pull myself together, I decided that I was going to live my life the way I wanted to. I was going to be free and enjoy every day and every experience as much as possible, and I was going to learn all that I could about anything and everything. I felt as if I finally had started to see how big life is, and I wanted savor it all.

In order to really survive and continue our lives, we need to have that kind of long-term, big-picture view. Look past the current moment, no matter how awful it is, and know that it won't last. It will end, and after it does, you will be somewhere better, and the worst part of the experience will be behind you. Then you can tackle the next challenge.

For me, the next hurdle to reclaiming my life was learning how to get other people to see me as a person and not as a statistic or a stereotype. I didn't want people to define me by my injuries. Yes, that experience is a part of me, but it's not what I want people to remember about me. I'd prefer they know me by my accomplishments, my actions, and my words. I want everyone to know me for what I do, because that's what defines how I survive and who I am.

Unfortunately, some people, even after they finish the rehab process, never really get on with their lives. They just sit at home and channel surf, watch movies, and play video games—and that's all they ever do. Life becomes about what happens to them, not what they're doing. They dwell on that one moment when they got hurt, on whatever event changed their life, and then they act as if it's not worth even trying to do anything else.

"I can't," they say. "I can't do what I want to do the way I used to do it, the way I want to do it." They give in to that poisonous idea: *I can't*. I hate that phrase. It makes me sad and angry to think of how many lives have been wasted because of that stupid, self-defeating expression.

Part of what holds people back, I think, is the failure to really accept what has happened to them. At first, I wasn't able to accept the change that had been inflicted on me. I was aware of it, I acknowledged it, and I thought this was enough. It wasn't. On some fundamental level, deep inside, I was still fighting against the truth. I was angry at what had happened, and part of me wasn't ready to let go of the life I'd had before being blown up.

Learning to accept things was a lesson I learned from another triple amputee, a guy named Joey Bozik. He had been hit one year and four days before I was. He had already endured everything I was just starting to experience—waking up at Walter Reed, learning what had happened to him, slogging through rehab, you name it. So, I started asking him questions. When I first met him, he wasn't yet walking on his own, but he was getting close to doing it, and he was definitely a lot further along in the process than I was.

I met Bozik only after I had begun my rehab program because

114

when I first arrived at Walter Reed, he was away on leave. During my first few weeks in rehab, I felt kind of lost. All the exercises seemed pointless. But after Bozik returned to Walter Reed and we got a chance to talk, he helped me by telling me something no one else could: "Once you *accept* it"—meaning my whole situation, getting blown up and having to rebuild my life—"once you own what has happened to you, only then will you be able to move on. If you want to heal, you need to *accept* it."

"I have." I waved off his advice as if I knew what I was talking about, but I really didn't understand what he was trying to tell me. I think I just wasn't ready at that moment to understand what "accepting it" really meant. It wasn't as simple as acknowledging the facts of what had happened. It wasn't about realizing that my life had been changed and could never again be the way it had been. It was deeper than that. What Bozik was trying to teach me was that I would never be able to be whole again until I found a way to work through my anger, my sense of loss, and be okay with who I'd become. I needed to let go of my longing for the man I used to be and learn to be happy being the man I am.

My epiphany didn't happen all at once, but I know where the breakthrough began.

Walter Reed can be a very inspiring place to visit. It's really uplifting to walk through there and see so many of the soldiers' great attitudes. But after spending months living there and seeing the sheer volume of patients that flows through that place week after week, it began to depress me. It made me realize I needed to experience real life again. One day I reached my breaking point. I said, "Mom, I'm going crazy! I need to get out of here! Let's go somewhere."

"Where do you want to go?"

"Vegas!"

An hour later, she had us on a plane to Las Vegas, which was great because my best friend Sarah lives there.

For one weekend, I stopped obsessing over my life and my rehab, and I just had fun. I did what I wanted to do, and I tried new things. I started living again.

My mom, Sarah, and I walked the Strip, went shopping, and gambled. I like craps and blackjack, so those are mostly what I played. I rented a scooter so I could get around on my own. It had a captain's chair with two armrests. The handlebars were a single lever. If you pushed on the right side, you'd go forward. Push on the left side and you'll go backward. Simple, right?

When visiting the craps tables, I had been parking sideways, which takes up a lot of space and crowds out other players. I felt bad about that, so I thought, *You know, the chair pivots on a dime. Let me see if I can back the scooter up to a table and then pivot to face the table so that I only have to take up one spot.*

I was parked at a craps table as I had this notion. Turning in my seat to look back, I saw another game in full swing right behind me. But as I turned my body, I accidentally pushed one of the armrests against the handlebar. The chair clicked into gear and shot forward with me riding sidesaddle and unable to reach the controls.

Directly ahead of me, standing in the path of my runaway scooter, was an unsuspecting guy at another craps table. I slammed straight into him without so much as a "Look out!" The poor guy wound up pinned against his table, bent like a boomerang and howling like crazy, while the scooter burned rubber on the carpet like a hot rod being primed for a drag race.

116

Between shouts of "Oh my God!" I tried to stop the scooter, but because the armrest was jammed forward, I couldn't get the thing out of gear. Within seconds I was pushing this poor guy and an entire craps table across the casino floor.

Finally, I pulled back the armrest and backed up off the dude, but by then the pit boss had come over to see what the hell was going on. "I'm so sorry," I said, over and over again.

Word must have spread about my big crash, because I swear the rest of the weekend no one came with ten feet of me, like I was driving a bumper car in a china factory. Maybe I should have put a "student driver" sign on the back of my scooter.

Another first for me during that trip was a visit to an oxygen bar. The notion of paying to breathe something that's free everywhere you go seemed weird to me, but I was curious, so I checked it out. The place I went to had different flavors of oxygen. Yes, *flavors*. Anyway, I sat down and strapped a respirator tube under my nose. For ten minutes I camped out and savored a noseful of really expensive air. Every few minutes the bartender came back and asked me if I wanted to try a different flavor. Then she put this spiderlike metal device on my head, and it started massaging my scalp while she rolled a ball-bearing massage bar across my back.

I never thought I'd enjoy paying for air while wearing a steel spider on my head, but I have to admit, it was kind of fun.

When I went back to my hotel room, I jumped into a Jacuzzi that's bigger than most New York apartments, filled it, and treated myself to a hot soak. Leaning back, surrounded by warm froth, I admitted to myself, *Yeah . . . this is all right. I can do this, no problem.*

My mom and I returned to Walter Reed the following Monday. That was the first time since being blown up that I really felt as if

I was able to put things right in my head. Sitting by the reflecting pool outside the Malone House, I thought, *If I had fun while I was in Vegas, and for just a little while I was able to stop thinking about what happened to me, why not just have fun all the time?*

That was when I began to accept the new status quo in my life. I decided, *This is it. I'm going to do everything in life that I possibly can. I want to be somebody.*

That three-day jaunt to Las Vegas had been the turning point for me, but the only thing that had changed was my outlook. I had gone from seeing my rehab as a chore that I needed to do so that I could adapt to the new life I had to lead, to seeing it as the first step on a journey to the life I wanted to live. Just by changing how I saw myself—by accepting who I was, inside and out—I discovered that I didn't merely have to *exist* as a triple amputee, I could really *live* as one. It was a choice, and I made it.

I chose life.

When I think of people who are taking the wrong approach to surviving, I think of homeless veterans I see on the streets. I know this might sound harsh, but when I see a veteran wearing filthy rags, sitting on a sidewalk, and begging for change because he's obviously a drunk or an addict, even if he's an amputee, I think his situation is completely his own fault.

Before you run me out of town with torches and pitchforks, let me explain.

Maybe life dealt guys like this a lousy hand. They lost their job, the Veterans Administration wouldn't help them, or they lost a loved one or got kicked out of their house. I know that these things happen, and they're devastating. I'm sympathetic to that—but only up to a point.

Once these veterans start living on the street, that's a *choice*, and it's a bad one. I don't give money to people like that when I see them begging. "Go get a job," I tell them. I don't say it to be a jerk or because I'm selfish. I just want these people to help themselves first.

Military experience is a great thing to have on your résumé. Potential employers sit up and take notice of it. I'm not saying some ex-grunt can walk into a Fortune 500 company and become a CEO, but there's no excuse for not seeking at least an entry-level job and working your way up. In some industries, like food service and retail, a military background can get you in the door at the assistant-manager level. There's no shame in managing a fast-food joint or a knickknack shop in a mall. A job is a job. As long as you're taking steps to better your life, you can do any job with pride.

But when I see people wearing the tattered remains of their uniforms while sitting in their own filth, asking for pity, it makes me angry. I can't respect someone who would rather scrape through each day looking for a drink or a fix to dull their pain than muster the discipline to fight through it and take back their own life.

It makes me crazy when I see people who gave up after the military spent years trying to teach them to be self-sufficient and lead people. Even if you're just a buck private, from day one you're still being taught the basics of leadership. You never know who's going to be called upon to lead in a combat situation, so everyone is expected to be ready if the duty falls upon them.

So why would someone who has that kind of valuable training

choose to just sit on the street and ask for charity? That's *not* what a soldier is trained to do. A soldier is supposed to get up and find a way forward, no matter what.

I want to tell each of those homeless vets this: It is not impossible to fix your life, but you won't get any better, and your situation won't improve, if you keep repeating the same broken pattern of behavior. Stop doing what doesn't work and try something new. Visit a homeless shelter and get a shower. Go to the Salvation Army and get some clean clothes. Sign up with a temp agency and go on job interviews until someone hires you. Stay at the shelter until you save enough for an apartment. Step by step, take your life back.

Bottom line: If you're in a bad situation, you need to pick yourself up and do something about it. Don't wait for solutions to come to you. Make your own answers.

Giving yourself over to any kind of a crutch—whether it's booze, drugs, pity, lashing out in anger, or whatever you might use to avoid accepting responsibility for your life—is the wrong approach to surviving. Taking that road, no matter how satisfying it might feel in the moment, will only make you weaker. It will make you less than you are, less than you deserve to be.

There are ways of getting help so that you can start your life over again. So why don't people take advantage of those opportunities? Pride, maybe. They're afraid of being shamed in front of people they care about, or looking foolish in public. Either one is a lame excuse for not doing the right thing. If there are people who care about you, then you're doing them more harm by not getting help, and your pride doesn't matter. If all you're afraid of is looking bad to people you don't know, why do you care about the opinions of strangers in the first place?

People who are dependent on booze or drugs or any other addiction let everything else fall away until that's the only thing in their lives. Others might not be addicted, but they've lost their job or their wife or their legs, and they still spend the rest of their lives shrinking away from those problems. You can't just live in a little hole in the center of your life. There's so much out there when you live a full life instead of a life you allow to collapse around you. Don't define your whole life by these incidents, don't just exist from moment to moment. Break out of that corner you've painted yourself into. Look around at the whole wide world, not just the pain you're feeling. No matter how bad your problems are, they're small compared to your potential. Live large.

I know it won't be easy. There are all kinds of things standing in your way—pain, exhaustion, pride . . . but they all come down to one thing: fear. Fear of suffering, of failing, or being embarrassed, of never getting better. That barrier is there, and it's very real.

My point is, you need to push through it. Courage isn't the opposite of fear; real courage is being afraid and doing what you need to do despite knowing that you're scared. It doesn't matter what you're afraid of. Once you conquer it and come out on the other side, you're going to feel so much better because that ordeal's behind you, and because you can really feel like you've accomplished something. It's an essential part of feeling like you're moving on, and doing things, and becoming a functioning part of society.

So stand up and find a way to live. You owe it to yourself.

When you can do that, you'll be a true survivor.

9

LIVE, LOVE, THRIVE

There are very few events that I can truly say have changed my life. Getting blown up was one, and being on the cover of *Esquire* magazine was another, but kissing Caroline was the big one: that was the first time I really fell in love. I'd been with other women, but I'd never felt anything like that before. It turned out to be less than I hoped for and more than I expected. I don't know if that makes sense, because I still don't really understand what happened between us. But I know I loved her and that going through all those ups and downs taught me things that are still around even though she's gone. I don't regret it. It's worth it, putting yourself out there.

It started in early August 2005, when I was home on leave during my second tour of duty in Iraq. My family and I were on vacation in a little town in Wisconsin. We had a house there, right on Lake Michigan. One night we went out for dinner at a pizza place nearby. There were a lot of us, so we sat outdoors, at a long picnic table on the restaurant's screened-in porch. My twin brother was sitting across from me.

"Let's get some beers," I said.

Bobby waved over our waitress. She was a bit taller than me, with blue eyes and a lean, athletic figure. Her dirty-blond hair had red and white ribbons braided into it. The moment I saw her, all I could think was, *Wow—she is unbelievably hot.*

Her name was Caroline.

My family and I ordered a round of drinks. Caroline came back a few minutes later, carrying them on a tray. I couldn't stop looking at her as she handed them out, one by one. Then she stepped behind me, picked up my beer, and tried to reach over and around me. The glass slipped from her fingers and landed upright on the floor behind me. Its contents erupted in a cold wet blast right up my back, under my shirt.

I jumped up. "Holy shit!"

Caroline looked almost as surprised as I felt. "Oh my God," she said, struggling to clean and apologize at the same time. "I'm so sorry! That never happens to me. I don't know what happened!" Her face was red with embarrassment as she wiped spilled beer from the floor and my part of the picnic bench. "I *never* drop beers. Never, I swear."

It might seem like a strange way to break the ice, but she and I spent the rest of the night flirting with each other—trading smiles and little jokes, that kind of thing. I knew there was something special happening between us, so I asked when she would be working again.

That week, I went back to the restaurant . . . Five times.

I made a few of those return visits with friends, but I also went by myself a couple of times, and those were the times when I really got to talk with Caroline and learn a bit about her. One thing I learned was that she liked horseshoes. I didn't think to ask why. I was just so excited to have discovered something personal about her that I went out and bought us each a horseshoe charm on a chain. Mine was plain silver and hers was encrusted with tiny jewels. At least they looked like jewels. I didn't spend a ton of money, but I just wanted to give her something, even without any special occasion. It had only been a week, but I was falling hard and fast. When you feel like that, you don't always think about if the other person is in the same place you are, you just go for it.

After I gave her the charm, I invited her to a party I was throwing at my family's vacation house that Friday night. "Yes," she said, "I'll come! I'll be there. I just have to go to this other thing first at a bar on the other side of town."

I nodded and played it cool. "Okay. Just swing by after you're done there."

Friday night, everyone was having fun at the party, and I lost track of time. Around midnight, I noticed that Caroline hadn't shown up yet. I was really bummed out. *She's not here! She's not coming!* I couldn't believe she would blow off my party, especially because I was leaving the next day—I was going to meet my best friend for a week in Las Vegas before my leave was over, and then I was going back to Baghdad. That night was my last chance to see her, so I wasn't going to give up that easily. I made my friend Robi drive me over to the bar because I had been drinking and was in no shape to get behind the wheel. The place was only three minutes away, but I knew better than to drive in my condition.

Robi drove me to the bar and waited while I got clumsily out of his car. I guess I'd had a bit more beer than I realized. He got out, circled around, and steadied me—I don't know if it was just about the beer or also about being all wound up about Caroline standing me up. I slapped a hand on his shoulder. "All right, man, listen: if I'm not back out in fifteen minutes, you can leave without me."

Robi nodded. "You got it." He gave me a hug, slapped my back, and gave me a helpful push toward the door. "Go get 'er."

I staggered inside the bar and looked around for Caroline. At first I didn't see her anywhere, and I started to get worried. Taking my time, I pushed through the crowd to the back of the bar, but still I didn't see her, so I started working my way back toward the front door. By the time I got there, I had concluded that Caroline either hadn't been there, or had left earlier and I'd missed her. I was one foot out the door when I glanced to my right and saw her standing there. I shouted, "Caroline!" She looked right at me, her jaw slack with surprise.

Then she smiled. "What're you doing here?"

"You've gotta come to my party!"

"Why not stay here? We can get a few beers." That's when I finally realized that maybe the whole thing wasn't quite as special for her as it was for me. At least not yet. I had to get her back to my place somehow, get some private time with her.

"No, it's *my* party. If I'm not there, my drunk friends'll trash my house." Not the greatest line, but she agreed to come with me.

Robi was long gone by that point, so Caroline drove us back to the house. When we pulled into my driveway, we saw that the party was starting to wind down. We got out, walked out back to the bonfire, smoked a cigarette, and then we went back to the car. That's where we stayed, all night, just talking—about me, her, us . . . about everything and nothing.

It was a gorgeous night, warm and clear. There were so few streetlights out there in the boondocks that it got almost perfectly dark at night, which made it possible to see more stars than I'd ever imagined. Out in the middle of nowhere, with the world around us so immaculately black, the moon seemed ten times brighter. It was amazing.

That perfect night was the first time we kissed.

As soon as I kissed her, I *knew* it was love. It was like having fireworks go off in my heart. She was *the one,* and I felt it. Before that night I'd suspected it, I'd hoped for it . . . and when I kissed her, I knew for sure. She was the one for me.

That was as far as we went that night, but it changed me. I knew I'd never be the same.

We said good night as the sun came up, and then I got out of the car and watched her drive away. The last thing I wanted to do that morning was leave her, but my flight left for Vegas later that day. The week went by too fast and then I flew back to Iraq and rejoined my unit.

Caroline and I talked on the phone as often as we were able, and we traded e-mails all the time. Whatever I was feeling or thinking about each day, I put it in my e-mails to her. I wasn't holding anything back.

Roughly five weeks later, two of my best friends in the Army got killed by a roadside IED. That shook me up bad. I couldn't understand why great guys like them had died while I had gotten away with barely a scratch after one and a half tours in downtown hell. "Why them and not me?" I sent that off to my mom, a couple of friends, and Caroline. Looking back, I suppose that was one of those moments that people are referring to when they say, "Be careful what you wish for—because you just might get it."

The next morning, I got blown up.

After I woke up at Walter Reed, I didn't want to talk to Caroline. I didn't want her to see what had happened to me, so I stopped answering her e-mails or taking her calls. She didn't give up on me, though. She kept sending me e-mails, and my mom read them to me while I lay in bed. I never asked to send a reply. What was I going to say? I had no words for what I was feeling. I should have known better. I'd been pouring everything out to her for a couple months now and she'd stuck by me long distance and everything. But on some level, I guess I hoped that if Caroline never saw me again, she would always remember me the way I was, and that part of me would still be alive—it would still exist in her memory. It sounds crazy to me when I say it like that, but at the time I still hadn't really accepted what had happened to me. I didn't want her to see me like this. Or maybe I didn't want to see her seeing me like this, in my hospital bed after being blown to pieces. It would be that much more real to see it reflected in her eyes. I couldn't do it.

Unfortunately, I didn't understand that I was hurting Caroline with my silence. I was too wrapped up in my own pain and loss to think about her feelings. After all, she'd been putting herself out there for me while I was in Iraq. That couldn't have been easy for her back home in Wisconsin. Some folks would say my reaction was understandable, given the circumstances, but I'm not sure that makes it right. It explains how I was behaving, but it doesn't justify it.

She flew out to Washington, D.C., to visit me in the hospital, which was pretty amazing considering the way I'd been treating her. Once she was standing in front of me, I couldn't not talk to her. I saw that she was wearing the horseshoe charm necklace I had given her. That was the first time I'd noticed that mine had been lost in the explosion. She had brought me a photo of the two of us. It was inside a store-bought frame whose edges she had decorated with the red and white ribbons she'd been wearing in her hair the night we met.

Then she took my hand, and I knew that it was okay for her to see me, because when she looked at me, she didn't see my missing limbs or my scars or my burns. She saw *me*, the *real person*, and the way she looked at me made me realize that in her eyes, I was still the same guy she had kissed on that perfect night by the lake. I was still Bryan. I'd thought that she would see me the way I was seeing myself, seeing only what was missing. But she saw the person she had fallen in love with. I realized that if you assume people see nothing but your flaws, you can force them to see you in your worst light. That's what I'd done to her all the time I didn't answer her e-mails. If someone is kind enough, if they love you enough to see beauty in you, do yourself a favor—see yourself through their eyes.

After her first visit, we began dating. Over the next six months, she made several trips out to Walter Reed to spend time with me. Our whole relationship consisted of us being together at the hospital. Or going out to dinner at a nearby Mexican restaurant.

For the longest time, though, I thought I was only half a person—half a body. I thought that mattered. It really doesn't. Being with Caroline made feel whole again, like a real person, not just half of one. It wasn't any one thing she did or said that made the difference. It was all the little moments, like when we were riding in an elevator—me in my wheelchair and her standing beside me—and then I'd glance her way and see her staring at me. At first it seemed weird, but then I realized she wasn't gawking at me. It was as if she was radiating love and understanding, and it felt good just to bask in it, like sitting in the sunlight.

I never told her that. I don't know why. Back then those feelings were all still so new and raw that I didn't really know how to put words to them. Now I realize she really needed to hear those things from me.

The unconditional quality of Caroline's love for me after I came home from Iraq helped me feel at ease with who I had become. I couldn't have asked for anything more than that.

What I loved—and still love—about Caroline is that she doesn't just *talk* about doing things, she *does* them. She sees the potential in everything around her; she perceives things and people not as they are but as they could be. To give you an example, she had some funky old window shutters. She was going to throw them away but thought they looked too cool to waste, so she built a coffee table out of them.

I was so impressed when she showed it to me. "You built that?"

"All it took was a hammer and some nails," she said. "Simple."

"Awesome."

She lives the way I like to live. I was convinced I'd found the perfect woman.

Then, all at once, everything seemed to go wrong. I had planned a weekend away from Walter Reed, a trip down to Fort Hood, Texas, to see my Army buddies. I invited Caroline to meet me down there so I could introduce her to my friends, and she accepted. This was a really big deal to me. I've been through life and death with these guys; in some ways, I'm closer to them than I am to my family. I wanted them to meet Caroline because I was in love with her. I caught a Friday-afternoon flight, and Caroline was supposed to meet me in Texas the next day.

Saturday arrived, but Caroline didn't.

I called her and asked what had happened. She said she had lost her ID, and that without it she couldn't board the plane. I couldn't believe it. I was devastated. It was kind of like the night she didn't come to my party. But this time, instead of going after her, I got pissed and didn't talk to her for days. More not talking on my part.

Later, I learned that despite telling me she was twenty-one years old, Caroline was, in fact, only nineteen (not that I would have cared). I'm not sure this had anything to do with her not getting on the plane, but learning she had been lying to me made me really angry. It hurt me to think that she didn't trust me enough to tell me the truth. I didn't think about all that time I hadn't answered her e-mails.

I broke up with her—she'd say she broke up with me—and we shut each other out for nearly a year. Then we started talking again. That led to us hanging out, though not exactly dating as we had been. I made a trip up to Wisconsin and learned that she had started dating a new guy. I met him. He seemed like an okay dude.

Two weeks later, she came to visit me in D.C. for a weekend. During that trip, I asked her, "What's the deal with us? I know you've got this new guy, but you've only been with him three months, and I think you know that what you and I have is special."

"You really hurt me when you stopped talking to me," she said. "I'm afraid that when you go traveling, one day you'll leave and not call me anymore."

"Why would you think that?"

"You did it before."

"What? When I was mad at you for a few days because you didn't come to Texas? What'd you *think* I was gonna do?"

The next thing I knew, we were kissing. Maybe it was something I said, but I doubt it.

All these feelings I'd had when I first met her came rushing back, and for a moment I actually believed that she'd choose to stay with me, that we'd be together again.

I was wrong. Everything turned weird between us, and she went back to Wisconsin.

I sent her an e-mail and poured my heart out, told her exactly how I felt about her and how much she meant to me. She never replied to that message.

More time passed, and we made plans to get together again. She was going to come visit me for St. Patrick's Day so that we could have a few beers together. The day before she was supposed to arrive, she called to say she wasn't coming.

"Why not?"

"My boyfriend read your last e-mail. He says I'm not allowed to hang out with you anymore, and he doesn't want me talking to you either. He doesn't think it's a good idea."

"A *good idea*? All I want to do is have a beer with you on .St Patty's."

"Sorry." She hung up.

I wasn't done talking, but I knew she wouldn't take any more of my calls, so I got in my car and drove up to Wisconsin. I pulled up to the bar where she worked . . . and then I sat in my car, wondering what the hell to do next. I wondered, *What if her boyfriend's there? Damn it, I'm sure he is. Where else would he be? That would be just my luck.* Finally, I decided it didn't matter. I hadn't driven all that way just to wuss out, so I got out of my car and went inside. And, as I'd expected, Caroline and her boyfriend were sitting together at the bar. *Of course they are.* I had no idea what to say, so I climbed up onto a bar stool next to them and ordered a beer.

Caroline looked at me, dumbfounded. "What are you doing here?"

"You said you'd have a beer with me on St. Patrick's Day, so here I am. All I want is a beer." I nodded at her boyfriend. "Hey. What's up?" He didn't look happy to see me.

The conversation was tense, awkward, and sparse as I drank my beer. To be honest, there wasn't much to say. When my mug was empty, I set it down, said my farewells, and left.

That was the last time I ever saw Caroline, but not the last time I spoke to her.

A few months after my unannounced visit to Wisconsin, we spoke once via text message. It didn't go well. At the end of it, I got fed up and told her, "Fine, I'll just lose all your info. Consider yourself deleted." I purged her information from my phone and computer.

Whenever I go back up to my family's vacation house, I find myself thinking about Caroline, and I ask myself, *Why did I let things happen the way they did? Why didn't I do this or that differently?* I hate feeling that way, because I don't believe in living with regrets. Yet every time I go out to the house on the lake, I kick myself and grumble, "Son of a bitch. This is not the way this was supposed to work."

I've lain awake more nights than I can count, asking myself

over and over, *How did my relationship with Caroline go so completely wrong? How did I meet the greatest, most beautiful girl in the world, fall in love with her, and then lose her?*

Well, at long last, I think I've unraveled the mystery and found the answer: I'm an idiot.

When I was lying in my bed at Walter Reed and ignoring Caroline's e-mails, I showed no trust in her, in the feelings she obviously had for me. But she still stuck by me through those bad times. Even when I couldn't love myself, she still loved me. I kind of took that for granted. Even though we got through it, there were times I still held back from telling her everything. And that was wearing her down. I didn't pour it all out to her until that e-mail I sent her when she was already with her new boyfriend. I should have known how that would go over.

You might think after reading about my relationship with Caroline, that I'm a complete loser when it comes to women, but I'm really not. Ever since I finished rehab, I've had better luck on the dating scene than I ever had before I got blown up, and I owe a lot of that good fortune to the confidence I gained from my appearance on the cover of *Esquire*.

I never thought I was good-looking in any kind of way. But after so many strangers told me, "You have such presence," or "You have a good look," I began to take notice. During interviews, more than one reporter said to me something like "It doesn't hurt that you're good-looking, too." After a while that sort of constant positive reinforcement started to stick with me. That's how my confidence was built.

Soon it was the same thing with women telling me I was good-looking. At first it was only Caroline, but after her there were others. Women I had just met kept telling me that I was handsome or cute. I'd hear this and throw a funny look at them. "Really?"

"Absolutely."

After hearing it enough times, I began to think it might not be total bullshit.

Those little moments add up, and in the long run, they make a difference.

When I was interviewed by *Esquire*, I said that I thought my injuries had made me ugly. I don't think that way anymore. And traveling as a spokesperson for Quantum Rehab, I've had the chance to meet lots of people all over the United States. Becoming a public speaker gave a huge boost to my self-confidence. Once I learned how to talk to a crowd, talking to one woman in a bar or at a party didn't seem so intimidating anymore. Then I started to land acting gigs—on *CSI: NY, All My Children,* and *The Wire,* and in movies like *The Wrestler*—and I really began to believe that I wasn't some modern-day Quasimodo freak.

Esquire can't take all the credit for helping me make this transformation, though. The truth is, it all started with Caroline. She didn't judge me based on how I look or how many parts I have. She cared about who I am as a human being. Whether it's about looks or limbs, you can't put yourself down. You've got to believe in the good other people see in you. If you don't, then deep down you can't love yourself. And that will sabotage the relationships you have with people who do love you. You'll shut them out because you don't trust their love, you'll think that they can't love you for whatever stupid reasons you get stuck in your head.

The power of love is what makes everything else possible. That's why it matters. That's how Caroline made me into a whole person again. Sure, it hurt that I lost her in the end, but she brought me healing beyond what the doctors could do, and I will always owe her for that.

So don't be afraid to show your feelings to the people you love. And if someone wants to show you love, don't ask why—just accept it, because that's as good as life gets.

10

KNOW WHEN TO WALK ALONE

We all need help sometimes. When you start learning how to ride a bicycle, there's nothing wrong with using training wheels until you get the hang of it. Kids learning to swim in a pool where even the shallow end would be over their heads ought to start with an adult beside them to help keep them afloat, or with one of those funny-looking flotation vests. At any age, if you decide to take up parachuting, your first jump has to be with a qualified instructor, someone trained to help you out if something goes wrong. This is all common sense: if you're learning to do something potentially dangerous, you take a few precautions during the learning process.

There comes a time, though, when you have to take off the training wheels, leave the flotation vest on the beach, or jump out of the plane by yourself. Sooner or later, we all need to be able to walk alone.

I had friends at my side the first time I got on a skateboard after I left rehab. It's easy to wipe out on a skateboard even when you have all your limbs. For me to try it alone after such a radical change in my body would have been beyond stupid—it would have been insane. Once I got comfortable being back on the board, though, I didn't want anybody looming over me. After a certain point I knew it had to be about me, alone on the board, facing my fear.

Perched at the top of a skate ramp, ready to plunge straight down, I felt as if I had a half-million butterflies banging around inside my gut, slamming back and forth in my stomach. It was my choice to be there; I had put myself in that situation. Taking that risk was my choice, and I did it because I knew I'd hate myself if I didn't. But that doesn't mean I wasn't nervous as hell.

My body sent me crazy signals, like telegrams written on adrenaline: "What the hell are you doing, man?" Looking straight down that ten-foot wall, I couldn't help thinking, *It doesn't look this high from the ground.* I admit it: I hesitated. I knew that if I made one mistake, I could crack my head open on the cement.

That was my cue to just do it, that awareness of the challenge. That nervous feeling was telling me I was doing something exciting and I wasn't going to let my fear keep me from that. One push was all it took.

Gravity took over. My stomach lurched into my chest as I felt wind on my face—not a gust of natural wind, this was all about the speed of my body in free fall. My transformed body. Could I trust it? In a way, most of my skateboarding experience had been lost with my legs. For a few seconds that felt stretched by my fear, all I knew was the thrill of gaining momentum. Then my run panned out, and I coasted up the other side of the half-pipe before making a gentle arc back to the bottom.

My voice echoed off the concrete walls: "Yeah! I made it!"

Skating the half-pipe had just become yet another thing that no one could ever again tell me I couldn't do. I'd pushed my limits and gone further than I had expected. In a single moment, I had conquered a challenge I'd been afraid of—not the half-pipe, but my own body. From that moment on, I knew that I could trust myself again.

I found that moment deeply satisfying. It was exhilarating to push through my fear. I think it's probably like that for a lot of people, maybe for everyone. I'm not talking about a serious, irrational phobia, such as claustrophobia or a fear of snakes or something like that. What I'm talking about is a moment when you're afraid to commit to something that you really want to do, and then you do it anyway. And it doesn't have to be a physical challenge. Maybe you want to move to another city, or even another country. You're hesitant to leave your life as you know it, but excited about the possibilities of this new place, so you pick up and go. Or maybe you're thinking about changing careers, leaving what's comfortable but boring or unfulfilling. You take a chance and you find new opportunities and a passion for what you do. You're facing your fears and taking the leap. When you break through that psychological wall, it's *fun*. It gives you a rush like no other. It's a concentrated dose of life.

Could it all have gone horribly wrong? Of course, but that's no reason to avoid the experience. There's a difference between choosing to take a risk and wiping out, and having something happen to you that you can't control. And they're both better than just sitting on your ass playing it safe. If I go down a half-pipe and lose my balance and get laid out, that's my fault. But if, as I'm starting my run, my board breaks or it throws a wheel—that, to me, is fate. You can't control stuff like that. All you can control in those situations is how you react to them. Fate's a funny thing. You can take all the precautions you want—check all your stuff, make sure everything's tight, have a plan . . . but none of that matters if the ground falls out from under you. You can't prepare for everything. You can't control everything. Every once in a while you just gotta take a chance. You can't sit there wasting your life waiting until everything is perfectly safe or controlled. That never happens. If you behave like that, you'll never try anything new. So you gotta have faith. It could be faith in God, or in yourself, or in someone else, or whatever, but you gotta have it.

What matters is mustering the courage to leap—and being able to do it alone.

It can be difficult to know when you've had enough help and are ready to go solo. My opinion is that you should always push yourself to go further and work harder. Make your body and your spirit give just a bit more than you think they want to, and most of the time you'll surprise yourself. Whether the challenge ahead of you is physical, mental, or emotional, I've always believed that we rise to the challenges before us.

Part of the problem is that the people around me haven't always shared that faith. They all mean well, I think, but too many of them have no idea when to let me take care of myself. For instance, when I first came home to Illinois after finishing my rehab at Walter Reed, I invited people over to my house. A lot of them, instead of acting like my guests, started acting as if they were my hosts, there to serve me. Anytime I tried to leave the room to get something, one of them would jump up and run to get it for me. If I said I was hungry, they'd offer to get me food: "Do you want me to order some takeout? Or pick something up for you?" Some of them just walked into my kitchen, started cooking for me, and came back with plates of food. If I wanted to see them scurry like headless chickens, I'd point out that they forgot to bring me a napkin.

Before long, they were doing everything around my house: dusting, vacuuming, laundry, you name it. I couldn't get at any of my appliances because well-meaning friends and family members were always there running them for me. Eventually, I didn't even need to get up. For a while it didn't seem so bad. If I had been the kind of person who was content to let other people hand him things, I might have stayed like this for years.

The problem is, if you get used to being waited on, there's a price to pay. Sooner or later, the bill always comes due, and if you've gone soft while being waited on, you'll be in big trouble.

No matter how lovable you are, even the most generous people won't be your flunkies forever. They have their own lives and problems; they have school, jobs, and kids. One by one, they'll begin to show up less frequently. They'll all drift away, and one day you'll call out for someone to bring you a beer and there won't be anyone there to tell you that you've got two hands and four wheels, so you should go get it your damned self. And then what? You're so used to people doing everything for you that you can't do anything for yourself. What kind of life is that? You'd have no independence; you'd always have to depend on someone.

I first learned this lesson at Walter Reed. In rehab, a therapist will work with you for only so long. After a certain period of time, you have to figure things out for yourself. This is practical thinking at work. When you're learning to walk on prosthetic legs, for example, you don't want your therapist to help you up *every single time*. If you never learn to pick yourself up off the floor while you're in the clinic, how will you do it when you're out in the real world? Having too much help during therapy is actually counterproductive. The whole point of rehab is learning to live without training wheels. If you want your independence back, there is no other way to do it.

I'm not saying that accepting any help is a mistake. Only you can know for certain whether you're getting a needed helping hand or letting yourself be coddled. It's important to pay attention, though, because it can be very tempting to take the easy way when people keep offering it to you. Giving in to that temptation too often will only serve to undermine your progress and make you weaker, and that, in turn, makes you less valuable—both to yourself and to the people around you. Warning signs to look out for include moments when you ask yourself questions like *What do I do around here?* or *Why does everyone think I'm helpless?* If the thought of doing things by yourself—whether around the house or outside it—starts to seem too scary, that's another red flag. If you can't imagine leaving your house unless there is someone to go with you, then you've crossed the line from accepting help to being hobbled by kindness.

How do you keep from crossing that line? It can be as simple as opening a door.

When I'm in a public space, such as a shopping mall or a restaurant, I often have to deal with obstacles that most people take for granted: doors. For a regular person, it's easy: you walk up to a door, push or pull it open, and step through. In a wheelchair, that process is a bit trickier. I need to figure out which way the door opens, and on which side the hinges have been placed. If there are double doors, I need to choose which one to use, and that can depend on which way I need to go once I'm on the other side, the obstructions I have to navigate to reach it, and whether there are other people coming or going at that moment.

All this might sound complicated, but I've had a lot of practice, so it's actually not that big a deal for me. That said, if someone sees me coming and is nice enough to hold the door open for me so that I can just roll on through, that's great. It's just a nice moment of social courtesy, and I'm not some defensive jerk who gives people a hard time—"I can open the door myself!"—when they're just trying to be nice to me.

As long as you know that you can do it yourself, there's no harm in accepting courtesy and a helping hand from other people. It doesn't make you any less of a person, or make your accomplishments any less meaningful. It took me a while to learn this.

Imagine, though, if I always needed another person to open the door for me, everywhere I went. Suddenly I've become a loser who can be stopped dead in my tracks by a closed door. I might end up sitting there all day, waiting for someone to come along. How lame would that be? I'd be ashamed to be constantly dependent like that on other people.

Learning to make your own way isn't just about the little things that clutter up daily life. It's also about being allowed to fail, to make your own mistakes without other people shielding you from the consequences. I first saw this in rehab, when my therapists ran themselves ragged trying to prevent me from falling. They didn't understand that pushing myself past my limit was how I grow and learn—it was my way of healing. Their experience had conditioned them to see falling as a bad thing, because it might lead to a patient getting hurt, and it always resulted in them needing to fill out an incident report in triplicate. If I had to guess which one of those two consequences they were more worried about, it would be a toss-up.

What I had to explain to them was that I needed to fall, and I needed them to let me do it. They made a deal with me: I could push myself as hard as I wanted, as long as they could put down padded mats to cushion my landings. Knowing a good offer when I hear one, I agreed.

I believe that I recovered more quickly in rehab because I refused to be coddled. "No special treatment," I said to my therapists. "Don't let me off easy. I'm here to work." My mom respected this decision, too. She did all kinds of things to help me; she was always there when I needed her. I like to tell people that I've made it on my own, but on days when I was barely holding myself together, my mom was there—running errands, getting rental cars and driving me around, sorting out paperwork, and generally making sure that I was staying positive. What's important, though, is that she knew the difference between coddling and encouragement, and she never stopped reminding me to do what I had to do so that we could go home sooner rather than later.

Whenever I got frustrated or felt as if I'd hit a wall, my mom would turn the situation around on me. One time, after I had just started working with new prosthetics, I complained, "Mom, my new legs hurt."

"Yeah," she said, "but you're gonna get used to 'em, just like you did with your arm."

And she was always right. I guess it was a difference in point of view. I was seeing trees, but Mom had some distance, so she was able to see the forest. That's why she was able to help me find my way back out of that dark place whenever I felt like I'd gotten lost.

At the end of each day, though, she made sure that I was still doing the work of getting better. She was there to help me, not do it for me, and she made sure I never forgot that.

In fact, the only person at Walter Reed who ever tried too hard to shelter me was my roommate, "Sunshine." Whenever he saw me struggling to do something, he'd step in to do it for me, whether I'd asked for his help or not. Once he was involved, he wouldn't let me help or even do part of the work, he'd just take over—which was never what I asked of him.

I guess he thought he was doing me a favor, but the truth is, he was actually holding me back by preventing me from learning things I needed to know. It was frustrating, but dealing with Sunshine taught me another valuable skill: how to politely tell someone that I don't need their help. The key, I found, was to be calm, direct, and honest. "You know," I said, "I really appreciate the fact that you're trying to help me out, but I really need to learn to do some of this stuff on my own. Don't get me wrong. I'm grateful for the help, and I promise that if I need your help with anything, I'll ask. But unless I get some hands-on time with this stuff, I'm never gonna learn to get by on my own." I let him know that he was welcome to sit there, "supervise," and watch me work, and I asked him to step in if he saw I was about to hurt myself.

That was all it took. From then on, he eased up and let me get my hands dirty.

This can work both ways, of course. I think we all know what it's like to watch someone we care about as they struggle to cope with something difficult. The urge to get involved, to take over and save them, can be overwhelming. Even more difficult, though, is seeing a person you care about get weaker and start taking the easy way out. It might begin with little things, like asking you to do the occasional favor, or loan them a bit of cash "until payday," or tell a white lie to cover for them, just to "prevent a scene" or save their pride.

In cases such as those, when you see that you're being asked to coddle someone, you have an obligation—as a friend or family member—to say no. I'm not saying you should refuse every request for help. The time to become concerned is when you see it turning into a pattern. If you can predict each request this person will make before they actually say it, then it's a good bet the pattern is already established, and it's time to break it. You need to stand up and tell whoever it is that's taking advantage of other people's sympathy, "Knock it off. It's time to grow up and start taking responsibility for yourself again."

It won't be easy. Breaking that kind of news to someone you care about can make you feel like a monster. There's a good chance that no matter how diplomatic you are, they'll get angry with you. They might even holler at you and tell you to get out and not come back. There's nothing you can do about that. It might suck, but in such a circumstance, the person you're trying to help needs the cold hard truth a hell of a lot more than they need another favor. If you really care about someone, be brave enough to call them on their bullshit.

Now, even though some of my examples come from my rehab, I don't want you to think that I'm talking only about overcoming physical challenges. Independence takes a lot of forms: financial, creative, and emotional, to name a few. Making the transition from being a kid to being an adult doesn't happen overnight. It takes a lot of time and effort, and it usually involves weathering some pretty major setbacks. Finding your first full-time job is a big step; so is moving into your first apartment, or buying your first house. Greater rewards carry bigger risks, though. When the economy turns to crap, any one of us can wind up out of a job on a moment's notice, for any reason or even no reason at all. Sometimes, through bad luck or simple mistakes, money gets tight and bills start to pile up. These are real struggles we all need to learn to face.

It's our parents' job to teach us how to function on our own as adults in the real world. If your folks did their job right, by the time you leave home you should know how to balance your own checkbook, pay your bills on time, take care of your own home and car, and look after your own health. Sometimes, though, even that's not enough. When you're young and haven't had much time to work and save money, it can be hard to scrape up enough cash to pay all the fees and deposits necessary to secure a new apartment, or to come up with the down payment on a new house and also pay for all the inspections and closing costs. In that situation, receiving a loan or even a gift from your family to help you get settled and start your own life as a grown-up is perfectly reasonable. That's a helping hand, and there's nothing wrong with that.

On the other hand, if you're pushing thirty (or past it) and your parents are still paying your rent, you just might be a coddled brat. If you've got your first gray hair and someone else is paying for your car, you might be a modern-day princess. If you're old enough that you can't count to your age using just your fingers and toes, and you still collect an allowance, then pardon my French, but you're a goddamned parasite.

Owning your life is about embracing the risks that come with freedom. If you let other people do the hard things in your life—such as paying your bills, for instance—it won't be long before you start to believe, maybe subconsciously, that you're not capable of earning your own money. I've seen people like this, and it's kind of sad. They just float along from one codependent relationship to another, leeching off everyone around them while at the same time copping an attitude of total entitlement. If this sounds like you, listen up, because I have a news flash for you: the world doesn't owe you anything, and neither do I.

Yes, I know that's a harsh statement, but I think it's better to come at a situation with directness and honesty, even when the things I have to say aren't pleasant. The idea that I'm trying to get across to you is fairly easy to sum up: A person should earn his or her independence through hard work and sacrifice. Childhood has to end sometime because the world needs grown-ups.

Why is being able to stand up for yourself and get by without help so important? If you can't take care of yourself, how are you supposed to help make the world a better place for anyone else? I think the best, noblest thing that any of us can do is work to help improve the lives of others, in whatever way we can. That could mean volunteering to help feed the homeless or building homes for people displaced by natural disasters. It might involve helping to make sure future generations have clean air and water, or standing up to fight for the rights of people who are being treated unfairly.

If those seem overwhelming to you, there are smaller things you can accomplish every day. Being a good friend. An act of kindness for a stranger. Just think of some time when you were having a shitty day and someone did a little favor for you, and what a difference it made to your mood. I believe that the best way to make a world we can all share is to care more about what can do for others than about what others can do for us. I'm all for making a profit and enjoying the rewards that come from hard work, but I think there's more to life than bringing home more money than your neighbor.

People who can't take care of themselves, though, usually aren't in a position to do much for other people. A person who has been coddled becomes dependent; all he or she has been taught to do is take, consume, and demand more. How can people spoiled that way ever learn to give, sacrifice, and think more about others than about themselves?

This is why I'm such a hard-ass on this subject. It's why I want you to always push yourself to work harder, to learn to get by on your own strength, wits, and resources. It's the reason I want you to be the firm but gentle hand that guides your family and friends down the same path toward independence. Building a better world and a brighter future is going to take a ton of hard work by a lot of strong people.

I plan to be one of them—and I want you all standing by my side.

11

DREAM BIG

I've always been a little guy from a small town, but ever since I was a kid, I've had big dreams. After all, why dream small? Dreams are free.

My brother, Bobby, and I grew up racing from one dream to another so quickly that even we lost track. As little kids, we were always running circles around the apartment complex where we lived, pretending we were spies, FBI agents, or police officers. We always had Spy Tech toys. I was sure I'd grow up to be some kind of a James Bond secret agent or a Special Forces commando. All I wanted was to do cool stuff and play with cool things. That much hasn't changed from then until now.

As Bobby and I got older, we turned our energy to sports. I played baseball from when I was around eight until I was about fourteen. Then, right before I started high school, I broke my leg sliding into third base. After the fracture healed, I looked around at my options. I'd already done baseball for six years, so I decided to try something new and went out for wrestling and gymnastics. *Let's give it a shot and see what happens,* I figured.

It turned out that my brother and I were natural gymnasts. Fourteen is a pretty late age at which to start learning gymnastics, but Bobby and I competed in the Illinois state championships four years in a row. I was even considering trying out for a spot on the U.S. Olympic team.

Then my life took a detour.

Two weeks after graduation, my high school team was scheduled to compete in the nationals. I didn't feel like spending those two weeks training, so I told the coaches, "I want two weeks to myself. We've been practicing for the last few months. Now it's summer, and I want a two-week break." They gave me my time off, and I came back two weeks later. I ran through my whole practice routine, and everything went fine. I felt ready to take on the world.

I was cooling down when my girlfriend came in. She said, "Teach me how to do that flip-trick you do." The move she was talking about was a standing backflip followed by a front flip. The way it works is you do a standing backflip, but as soon as your feet hit the mat, you punch forward into a front flip so it's one smooth, fluent motion—one-two, *boom-boom!*

"Okay," I said. I hadn't done one in a few weeks, so I was a little rusty, but I was sure I could do it. She watched me act out the move in slow motion. "This is how you do it: first, you have to throw your arms upward as you jump up and back."

For some reason—perhaps because I was out of practice—as I

did the trick to show her what I meant, I jumped higher than I normally did. When I rotated in the air and extended my legs to kick off the floor, the floor wasn't there—I was still falling. So I kicked air and then hit. Hard.

Both my ankles rolled up into my shins.

I didn't break anything or tear anything, but I stretched out all my ligaments, and *goddamn*, it *hurt*. The doctor who treated me looked at me and shrugged. "I don't know," he said. "You may or may not be able to keep doing gymnastics. But you're going to have weak ankles for the rest of your life. And there's nothing we can do to fix that."

Just like that, my gymnastics career was over. I'd be lying if I said I wasn't a little bit disappointed, but on another level I was kind of relieved, because part of me was ready to move on to something new.

There are probably millions of people who have stories like that one. One moment they had gifts and dreams of where those talents might take them in life—and then, in the blink of an eye, they ended up with nothing. What separates life's winners from its losers is what they do after that happens. The losers spend their time looking backward, mourning what they lost and marinating in self-pity. Winners bid farewell to the lost dream and set their sights on a new one.

I can understand the temptation to sit around and relive one's glory days. It's like listening to songs that take you back to a time when you were young, especially happy, or in love. Playing those memories over and over in your head can bring back a bit of the moments that felt so good, way back when. The problem is those snippets of time don't last. No matter how good your memory, the glory dims and the cheering of the crowd fades away because those moments are in the past. When that happens, you have two choices. You can sit and mope and cry into your beer, or you can get up and start running down a new dream. I think you ought to get up and get going.

When you don't have anything to look forward to, you're not so much living as you are just existing. You're just going through the motions of your life. There's nothing wrong with that, if that's all you want. People can be very happy just going to work every day so they can pay their bills and maybe take a week's vacation at the beach. If that's all you need in order to feel fulfilled, to feel as if you've lived up to your potential, then it's a noble path. Where this can go wrong is if you're in denial. I know of many people who said they were happy with their day-to-day life, but in truth, they weren't. They just didn't know it until they took a moment to ask themselves what it was they really wanted. Don't fall into the trap of denying your dreams so often that you forget what they are. It's your dreams that give you the drive to improve yourself and strive for a better life.

In my case, finding a new goal didn't happen overnight. I had no idea what I wanted to do. All I knew for certain was that I wanted something easy. I didn't want to go to college. My uncle hired me to work with his company, painting houses and doing exterior remodeling jobs. It didn't take long for me to figure out that I hated this, but in the process I learned that I like working with my hands. I'm good at assembling complicated objects and machines—to me they're like puzzles, fun games to be sorted out—and I have a knack for building things. There are worse things that you can learn about yourself.

Finally, I got a job with the American Airlines ground crew at

O'Hare International Airport, and soon afterward I resigned myself to an ordinary life. *Here's my career,* I decided. *I can do this my whole life and make enough money to be just fine.*

To my surprise, my brother abandoned gymnastics and came with me to work at American Airlines, even though he hadn't been injured. It just goes to show you how close we are, and how competitive: Bobby figured if he wasn't going to be able to outperform me (As if he could! . . . Just kidding, bro), there was no point in competing at all.

I earned promotions quickly, and before long I was the youngest person ever to serve as a ground-crew chief at O'Hare International. All things considered, it was a really good job. For me, though, it wasn't enough. After three years there, I wanted more of everything—money, excitement, you name it. Living an ordinary life had been the fastest way for me to learn that I wanted to do anything but live an ordinary life. Unfortunately, I still had no idea what it was that I *wanted.*

I considered a lot of options before I hit upon the idea of joining the military. One thing that attracted me to the armed services was that I was curious about police work as a career. I'd always thought about being a cop, ever since I was a kid, and I realized that serving in the Army would let me try it without necessarily committing myself to it forever. I'd get on-the-job training, and I'd have a chance to travel and see different parts of the world. That sounded exactly like the life I wanted to be living.

Two years later, I was an MP deployed on my second tour of duty in Iraq. I'd learned a lot about myself in the Army. One insight was that I didn't like being a cop. At all. Another was that I was an adrenaline junkie, and that was what led me to my epiphany.

I had been keeping a journal while I was in Iraq. In it, I had been writing down all the different careers I might like to explore when I returned to civilian life. One night, me and my buddies were in one of the base's rec rooms, watching *Titanic* on DVD. During the final sequence of the ship's sinking, when it goes completely vertical and a man falls from a railing and pinwheels off the ship's propeller, one of my friends nudged me and said, "You know, that shot was an accident. The stuntman actually broke his leg when he hit the propeller. Cool, huh?"

Bing-bing-bing! The moment I heard that, I made up my mind. "Aw, dude, that's awesome," I said. "I'm gonna be a stuntman!" From that moment on, that was what I thought about whenever I had a free second to myself. It just felt right. Being a stuntman was a job that would combine everything I loved—I'd be able to work on movies and television shows, get a daily adrenaline rush from real danger, and do hands-on, physical work. Most of all, it was the first job I'd ever considered that sounded truly *fun*.

All I had to do was finish my hitch in the service, get my honorable discharge, and figure out how to get started. It was a perfectly simple plan.

Then, of course, I got blown up. That was not part of my plan. (And later I found out that my friend had been wrong . . . that shot was CGI. I was inspired to become a stuntman by a computer-animated character!)

After I got back stateside, I was told that the Veterans Administration was going to give me a certain amount of money every month for the rest of my life. Because of the extent of my injuries, I receive a pretty generous pension. If I had wanted to, I could have kicked back and lived a simple, nothing-fancy kind of life. I could have retired at the age of twenty-five.

I won't lie to you. For a while I considered it. Wouldn't you?

Once I finished rehab, I went home to Illinois to enjoy my retirement. I had thought I would enjoy the luxury of sleeping late every day and playing video games until my thumbs cramped. It didn't work out that way. For the first few weeks that I was home, I was bored. That's when I knew there was no way in hell that I'd be able to stand being retired.

I felt a need to stay active, to push myself to accomplish things. I wanted to be a player in the game of life, not just a spectator. I wanted to feel as if I had done something meaningful, useful, and, I hoped, also fun with my life.

Fortunately, I had started laying the groundwork for a new career while I was still in rehab. It didn't take me long to find an upside to my combat injuries. "Check it out," I said to my mom. "I'll make an even better stuntman now than I would've before!" I pointed out that a film crew could rig me with fake legs and a fake arm and blow them off—it would look awesome and completely realistic. Plus, I have a twin brother—that's always a plus for working in film and television, because it saves a ton of cash that would've been spent on special effects.

I still had no idea how I was actually going to break into the business, of course, but then I caught a lucky break. In what has become a common refrain in my life after the explosion, I was in the right place at the right time.

Walter Reed Hospital is visited frequently by a variety of celebrities. Some are politicians. Now and then, the soldiers there get to meet athletes. I recall one day during my rehab when I met three or four players from the Oakland Raiders football team. One of the other veterans handed them a football and they signed it. Things like that happened fairly often.

One afternoon I was in the clinic, practicing walking around on a new set of prosthetic legs, when a guest arrived. It was the actor Gary Sinise, who most people know from the television series *CSI: NY,* but whom all disabled vets know as the bilateral-amputee veteran Lieutenant Dan Taylor from the movie *Forrest Gump.*

I wanted to say hello, so I tried to walk toward him in a bit of a hurry. When I was still a few paces away from him, I tripped, lost my balance, and landed on his shoulder. He helped me up, and I stood back and flashed a big smile. "Sorry about that."

He looked back at me with wide eyes. "Holy shit! The *real* Lieutenant Dan!"

"No, no." I shook my head. "*You'll* always be Lieutenant Dan."

That made him smile. He sat down with me and we talked for about ten minutes. It wasn't a heavy conversation. We just shot the breeze and talked about . . . well, I don't really remember. I just know that it felt good to be seen as a regular guy by someone whose work I had admired and respected so much. Then one of his handlers tapped his watch, signaling Gary that it was time to go. He said a quick farewell, and then he was gone.

I didn't know it then, but I had just made a really important connection.

My next big opportunity was a phone call from an editor at *Esquire.*

"We're looking to do a story on a soldier," he said. "Can we do a story on you?"

"Sure. Why not?"

They sent a photographer and a writer to profile me for *Esquire* magazine's January 2007 "The Meaning of Life" issue. The writer and I talked for a few hours, and the photographer snapped a few shots of me, and that was it. After they left, I didn't give it another thought. I figured the article about me would probably get cut, anyway. Really, I think of myself as just another guy, and back then I was not a celebrity in any way. No one knew my name or who I was other than my friends and family and the people at Walter Reed.

Two weeks before the issue came out, I got another phone call from the editor.

"How ya doing?"

"I'm great. What's up?"

"The article came out great."

"That's nice. I don't think I'm all that interesting, but I'm happy it works for you."

"Awesome. Hey, we're gonna go ahead and throw you on the cover, too, just FYI."

"Huh? What? Whoa, wait a minute. I did some research on this special issue you're doing. You've got George Clooney and Robert De Niro and Scarlett Johansson, and then me? Are you sure about this? Really, I'm not anybody."

"No, trust us, it's gonna be great."

"All right," I said with a shrug. "It's your magazine."

Two weeks later, me and my Purple Heart were on the cover of *Esquire*.

That whole experience was a huge confidence boost, and it opened a lot of doors for me. Just seeing myself on the cover of

Esquire made me realize that all things are possible. Obviously there was some luck involved—sadly, there are a lot of wounded soldiers to pick from—but the important thing was that when I was called I said, "Yes." Right then, I knew that whatever I wanted in life, I just had to go after it. After that cover hit the stands, I shed all the fears that had been holding me back: *What if they don't like me? What if I'm not good enough? What if I fail?* I would have missed that chance if I had been worrying about this stuff, and really, do the answers to those questions even matter? So what if someone doesn't like me or thinks I do something wrong. All you can give is your best effort and keep at it. Once I crossed that psychological line, I never asked those questions again. You can't predict the answers, so why get hung up on the questions? Since then, my attitude has been "I'm going to do this. If it doesn't work, I will do something else." The key has been to keep moving—to go forward at all times, no matter what. How many times have you had the chance to do something new and passed it by for some reason? You're busy, or you're tired, or you're just nervous about something you've never done before. There are doors waiting for you to open them, so don't just walk by them like you've done every other day.

One of the first unexpected rewards of being on the cover of *Esquire* was that it landed me a new full-time job—one that I would never have thought to seek out for myself.

Dick McLane, the marketing director of Quantum Rehab, which manufactures manual and powered wheelchairs as well as other products for the disabled, had been searching for five years to find someone to serve as the company's spokesperson. When he saw me on the cover of *Esquire*, he thought that I might be the person he'd been seeking, or at least a contender, so he Googled me. Among the top hits were articles about my homecoming; one of the links pointed to the Web site of a major Chicago newspaper. When Dick clicked through to the story, he saw a photo of me in my power wheelchair. He looked closer, and then he found my phone number and called me.

When I answered, he introduced himself and said, "I saw you on the cover of *Esquire* magazine. First off, I'd like to thank you for your service."

"Thanks."

"So, I'll get right to the point: I saw a photo of you sitting on the Quantum 6000—"

"The what?"

"The power wheelchair."

"Oh. Yeah, okay."

There was a pause before he asked, "Well . . . how do you like it?"

He was being cautious. If I'd said that I hated it, he'd probably have shifted gears and started doing damage control. Luckily for us both, he didn't have to. "I really like it," I said. "My first power chair, at Walter Reed, was a rental, and it sucked. When I saw it, I was like, 'Are you kidding me? That's what I have to look forward to the rest of my life? Screw that.' So my dad picked out a new chair for me, and when he came back he said, 'Bryan, I got you the Mercedes of wheelchairs. It's built like a tank. It has six wheels. You're gonna love it.' And I do."

That was all Dick had needed to hear. "How would you like to be our spokesperson?"

"Huh?" It took me a second to realize I'd been offered a job. "Sure. Cool."

"Great," Dick said. "Welcome aboard!"

I had no idea what I was getting into, but I'm grateful every day for that call from Dick. Working as Quantum Rehab's spokesperson has been an education for me. I've learned about accessibility issues and the latest advances in technology to assist the disabled. It's given me the chance to travel and meet people. Best of all, it has given me a chance to be part of a company devoted to improving the lives of others and, in some cases, giving people their lives back.

For me, that's what it's all about. And it all started with my face on a magazine cover.

Here's a fun fact I've learned: being on the cover of a magazine gets you invited to lots of cool parties. Shortly after I debuted on the cover of *Esquire*, I started attending a number of events in the Chicago area. I soon found out that Gary Sinise is also from the area, and before long he and I started to notice that we were crossing paths on a regular basis. We started to greet each other like old pals.

He'd wave. "Hey, how're you doin'?"

I'd nod. "What's goin' on?"

Neither of us knew that thousands of miles away, gears were turning. One of the producers of *CSI: NY* had seen my magazine cover, and the photo had given him an idea for an episode. After the WGA writers' strike ended, he returned to his office and saw the copy of *Esquire* still sitting on his desk, and that got him writing again. When he was finished, he called me up. "I wrote an episode with a part in it for you. Think you can do it?"

"Of course I can!" Then I asked him, "Does Gary know about this?"

"No. Why?"

"Well, 'cause we're actually kind of friends."

"Ah . . . Let me go tell him."

The next day I got a call from Gary.

"Hey, man, what's up? I hear you're coming out to L.A.!"

"Yup, sure am."

"That's awesome. We're gonna have a good time. We should schedule a lunch."

Everything happened so swiftly that I could barely keep up. I spent eleven days in Los Angeles, hanging out with Gary in his trailer during the day. While I was there I gave him a framed picture of me and him that was taken during his visit to Walter Reed, and which I'd signed for him. He seemed to like it, and I thought that was pretty cool.

After I had the *CSI* gig under my belt, I landed a bit part on the HBO series *The Wire*, another in the Mickey Rourke feature film *The Wrestler*, and I even got to hang out on the set of *The Dark Knight* and watch them film the stunt in which a tractor trailer gets flipped upside down. I still loved the idea of doing stunts, but once I'd tried acting, I knew I wouldn't be satisfied working in the shadows anymore. I wanted to be a star.

That's another funny thing about dreams: they evolve. If you work at them and make them come true, they surprise you by getting bigger. It's as if you've reached the peak of a mountain, and only once you're standing on its summit are you able to see a higher crest that you weren't even aware of before that moment—and having seen it, you now want nothing more than to climb it and plant your flag there.

The more dreams I make come true, the more I realize that I don't have to limit myself to only one at a time. These days, I have my eyes on many prizes: I want to be an author, an extreme athlete, and an advocate for veterans and the disabled. Who knows? If I ever get tired of trying to change the system from the outside, maybe I'll run for office. Anything is possible.

What's particularly ironic about my story, of course, is that after I was blown up, most people assumed that the loss of my legs and left arm would limit my possibilities and restrict my options from that day forward. Instead, the opposite happened: getting wounded in Iraq and surviving as a triple amputee gave me notoriety, which led to media visibility. That led me to the cover of *Esquire*, which helped me land a guest spot on *CSI: NY* and so on.

I have been to so many places and done so many amazing things that would never have been possible had I come home uninjured from Iraq. If I had escaped the blast that day in Baghdad, and come home with all my limbs and fingers and toes . . . who would have noticed me? I wouldn't have been treated like a celebrity. There would have been no homecoming parades. No magazine covers. No acting jobs. No nothing. I'd be just another "lucky" guy who made it home from the war without too many visible scars—the ones that people notice most.

My point is that whether the things that happen to you are lucky or not depends entirely on how you think about them and what you make of the opportunities you're given.

Of course, I still daydream of having a whole body again. I look forward to the day when I can be like Steve Austin on *The Six Million Dollar Man* and run around on bionic legs. Until that day comes, though, I will keep making the most of the body I have.

There are days when I feel as if I have attention deficit disorder. I bounce through life like a pinball flying off bumpers. I need to have something to do. I can't just sit still. That's what pushes me forward, even now. Someday, when I am ready to kick back and enjoy the good life, I want to be proud of the way I've spent my time. Until then, I intend to chase my dreams, no matter where they take me—and that's exactly what I want you to do as well.

You see, dreams are like muscles. If you don't exercise them and make them grow, they will wither and waste away. So keep hope alive. Keep working to make your dreams a reality. Each small step you take will lead to another that is closer to your goal. Push yourself a little bit further each time, and never stop moving until you turn your dream into your reality.

No matter what roadblocks life throws in your way, you can find a way to keep going.

It might mean compromising on the definition of your dream; for instance, I can't run a marathon on prosthetic legs, but I could walk one if it was important to me.

It might mean asking for help. Check with your local or state government, or with private charities. You might find one that can help you acquire the tools you need to succeed. What matters is that you never surrender your dream, not even if you have to take really long, strange detours to reach your destination. Satisfy your hunger for life.

Once you do, you'll see that what your parents and teachers said was true: anything is possible if you are willing to commit yourself to it, mind and body, and do the work. Nobody believes this until they figure it out for themselves, and the reason why is that one can't be told the secret of success—each of us needs to learn it for him or herself.

Most important, don't listen to anyone who tells you that your dream is out of reach. *Nothing* is ever out of reach as long as you keep trying.

12

TALKING ABOUT IT

A big part of my job as the national spokesperson for Quantum Rehab is traveling the country, meeting people, and speaking to crowds. I tell hundreds of strangers at a time the story of how I got blown up in Iraq, and I confide in them about my rehab process. Anyone who knew me when I was a kid would find all this totally ironic, because I used to be shy. I was the quiet kid who kept to himself; I wouldn't talk to girls or introduce myself to other people unless they reached out to me first. The last thing I ever wanted to do when I was growing up was walk into a crowd of people I didn't know and start yakking away.

To be honest, this is still true, at least when I'm out and just minding my own business. I think of it as a personal issue, a matter of preference. Some people don't want to talk about themselves, and I'm one of those people. I don't like tooting my own horn because it makes me feel as if I'm bragging about how I've gotten to do all this cool shit, and that's totally not how I want to come off to people I've just met. So I tend to leave things out or let things slide.

Let me give you an example. Not too long ago I was at a diner with my former roommate Sunshine. While we were eating, he pointed out a decoration on the wall. It was a poster of a rock band that had been signed by one of its members, who had inscribed it with the message "Greatest milk shake I've ever had!"

I nodded at Sunshine and said, "That's cool," even though I had never heard of the band. I went back to enjoying my cheeseburger and figured that was the end of it. But you know how the waiter always comes by the table to ask how things are just when you have a mouth full of food? Kind of like that, Sunshine took it upon himself to summon the restaurant's manager just after a bunch of ketchup squished out of my burger into my lap. As I was trying to clean up, the manager walked up to the table. Sunshine pointed at the poster and then nodded at me as he said, "My friend ought to be up on your wall, too! He was on the cover of *Esquire!*" Apparently, Sunshine didn't realize that my glaring at him and shaking my head meant *Shut up, you're embarrassing me. And I have a lapful of ketchup.*

It's not that I'm ashamed of being on the cover of *Esquire.* The fact is, I'm really proud of it; it was a big moment in my life, one for which I'm grateful. But here's the thing: I don't run around crowing about it to strangers, because I figure it's not important to them and they have enough shit to deal with in their lives without feeling as if they also need to cater to my ego. That's not what I'm about. (In case you're wondering, a few days later, I mailed a signed copy of the *Esquire* cover to the restaurant's manager.)

Considering how much I hate being in the spotlight, it's kind of ironic that ever since the end of my rehab, I've been treated like some kind of minor celebrity by the media. The day I came home to Chicago after being discharged from Walter Reed felt like a holiday. I flew home on American Airlines, and when my flight landed, they did for me what they do for retiring pilots on their last flight: fire trucks shot their water cannons over the plane as it taxied in to the gate. As I got off the plane, an airline employee put Illinois sod grass on the jet bridge so that the first thing I stepped onto was Illinois soil, and as I was pushed in my chair toward the terminal, I saw that the jet bridge was lined with members of my family. Inside the terminal, three hundred employees of American Airlines were waiting; when they saw me, they gave me a standing ovation.

All that would have been enough to blow my mind, but there was more.

I left the airport terminal in a limo. Roughly halfway home, we pulled over into a rest area, where we were met by three hundred people on motorcycles. I saw all this and wondered, *What the hell is going on?* I was lifted out of the limo and placed into a police motorcycle's sidecar. Then we all moved out in one huge motorcade, down highways that had been closed all the way to my hometown of Rolling Meadows, where there was a huge parade in my honor. Afterward, we all ended up at some crazy bar. A few hours of drinking later, someone took my photo—after I was totally smashed and doing my best impression of Gomer Pyle. Naturally, that's the photo that ended up on the front page of one of Chicago's biggest newspapers.

I couldn't believe it. I still don't know what to say about that day except "Wow."

That wasn't my first brush with attention from the media, though. Rewind to a month or so before my homecoming blowout: as I was getting my affairs in order to leave Walter Reed, I was contacted by the producers of *Alive Day Memories: Home from Iraq,* an HBO documentary featuring actor James Gandolfini, star of *The Sopranos.* They wanted to know if I would be willing to be interviewed on camera about the day I was wounded and my experiences in rehab.

At that time I felt pretty down about myself. I had no idea why anyone would want to interview me. I didn't think I was that interesting. I just felt like a guy who'd been fucked up in Iraq. Ever since I'd come home, I'd been focused entirely on my recovery. In a way, I felt as if I was being selfish because I had shut everyone else out so that I could take care of myself. I had stopped going out of my way to help other people. I just worried about me, about getting myself back where I needed to be. The people around me—my family and therapists—kept saying to me, "You have such a great attitude, keep it up," but I couldn't stop feeling like a jerk.

With all those negative thoughts spinning around in my head, I wasn't sure if I wanted the kind of exposure that the documentary would bring, but I remembered another of my mottoes: "Try anything once." I agreed to the interview, and the producers made arrangements to bring me to New York City for the taping.

When my turn in front of the cameras arrived, my Army training kicked in. I had committed to do this, so I gave it my all. My fear vanished, and I let myself open up about everything: my wounding, my fear, my pain, and how I felt about the whole situation. The more I talked, the easier it got. I started dredging up details I hadn't shared with anyone before that moment. It was as if I was purging all this dark stuff from my soul, and it felt great. Best of all, I didn't care how I sounded or what anyone thought of me. I was just being honest. *If they like what I have to say,* I decided, *that's great. If they don't, they don't. It is what it is.*

It turns out that the producers had been kind of impressed by me. I learned later that they had interviewed thirty soldiers from different branches of the armed services, but they were only going to use ten of those interviews. When I found out that mine was going to be the first one shown in the finished film, it felt great; I was proud just to be a part of that project.

My role in this film helped me realize something important: talking about what had happened to me in Iraq was important not just because it helped me feel better about my life post-rehab but because it had the potential to help other people, too. By sharing what I had learned, I might be sparing someone else from the same fate, or serving as an example to someone going through the same kind of pain. I began to see that even though I had come home disabled, I could still be useful to others. My life could still have meaning.

After I was featured on the cover of *Esquire,* played a guest role on *CSI: NY,* and turned in a cameo for *The Wire,* my next opportunity to act in front of the camera put me somewhere I'd never expected to be: on a daytime soap opera. Along with two other soldiers who had been interviewed for *Alive Day Memories,* I was cast as part of an Iraq veterans' talk-therapy group on the daytime serial *All My Children.* It was an actual episode, scripted to fit into the show's ongoing story lines, but it was staged like a group inter-view. The producers asked us all to give natural answers, because we were all playing ourselves. We all got our turn in the spotlight, so to speak, but I noticed that the crew seemed to pay a lot more attention to me than to the other soldiers. That was when I realized that of all the veterans they'd recruited, I was the only one with real acting experience. I'm not saying that this made me any more genuine or my story any more compelling, because neither is true; the difference, I think, was simply that I felt more at ease being on camera and playing my part.

For whatever reason, I've never had a problem talking about what happened to me in Iraq. It's just part of my story, part of my life. I never had nightmares or flashbacks about being wounded. For me, talking about my experiences has always felt completely natural. I had accepted what had happened to me, and after I'd really opened up in the documentary, everything else seemed easy. I was moving forward with my life and felt proud of every new accomplishment.

I've also learned that I'm better at talking in front of a camera, or on a stage with lights in my eyes, than I am at speaking to a group of people I can see. In the first kind of setting, I no longer think about all the people who are watching and listening to me; instead, I focus on telling my story as if I'm speaking to one person. That focus makes it seem more personal, more like you're just telling a friend. When you're in front of a group, it's kind of artificial. I mean, how many people get up in front of a crowd to talk about their lives?

These days, when I sit for interviews, I put all my attention on the interviewer. He or she asks me questions, and I answer as if we're just shooting the breeze over a few drinks in a bar. As I've become more experienced, I've started answering questions a little bit more elaborately.

The funny thing is, in real life I'm still not comfortable being the center of attention. I hate getting awards, or making toasts, or being recognized when I'm just trying to enjoy myself. When I meet people who think I'm interesting, it takes a lot of effort for me to not look at them like they're out of their minds. I guess that's the fine line between talking about something and living with it, between enjoying the limelight and living with fame.

I don't regret my decision to take up acting, though—not for one second. When I was in rehab, I always said that I had no interest in going to talk therapy. Back then, I didn't feel as if I had anything to gain. It all seemed so touchy-feely, and I just didn't see the point. Clearly, though, there was a lot brewing inside me that needed to get out. I had things to say, I just had no idea how I wanted to say them—until I discovered how much I loved acting. What's weird, though, is that my acting career started with two things that weren't acting at all: the interviews by *Esquire* and with James Gandolfini for *Alive Day Memories*. Opening up and talking about my experiences paved the way for me to try acting, and acting has helped me put enough emotional distance between myself and my experiences that I can now talk about them on a regular basis. I don't have to feel like I'm being all sorry for myself and whining to a therapist, but I can still get those feelings out in the open, and in a way that it can help or entertain other people.

But one thing I always worry about is that after hearing my story, my audience will go away thinking that's all I am—that being blown up and going through rehab is all there is to know about my life. I usually don't have time during my speaking engagements to get into all the fun stuff that I've done, such as acting or taking up skateboarding and quad riding, so if there's one thing that I want people to keep in mind after they meet me or see me speak, it's that the story of my life didn't begin or end on the day I was blown up or when I finished rehab. I was a person before I went to Iraq, and I like to think I'm a better person since I came home. My life can't be defined by an explosion or the fact that I survived it.

The day I was wounded in Iraq and the months I spent in rehab at Walter Reed are just middle chapters in my story—one whose best chapters, I believe, have yet to be written. You don't need something as big as getting blown up to feel this way. We all have our setbacks. Bad shit happens to people, and you need to dust yourself off and get back in the game. If not, you're just settling for the way things are. Some people never recover from this kind of stuff, and that's sad. Here I am, I've gotten to do some really cool things in spite of—and because of—something horrible that happened to me. And I just keep looking forward to even more amazing things in my future. That's what everyone needs to do.

Obviously not everyone gets to be up onstage or in front of a camera. But as fun as that stuff was, it's really not necessary for what's important. All I was doing was being myself, sharing my story as honestly as I could. Whether you're doing that in front of a camera or a crowd or to just one person doesn't make a difference; what's important is how you feel and how you make others around you feel.

But all that sharing-emotions crap is hard. Talking about your fears and disappointments can make you feel vulnerable. A lot of

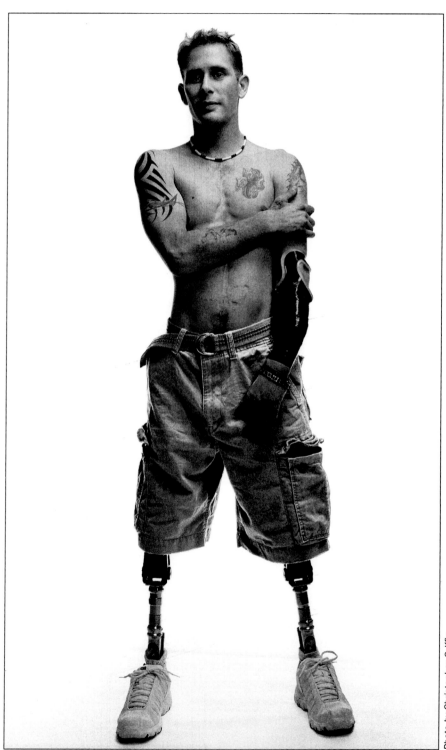

Me in my Little League uniform at eight years old.

Above Left: Winning first-place district wrestling title
Above Right: Mom and her twins, me and Bobby

Our family

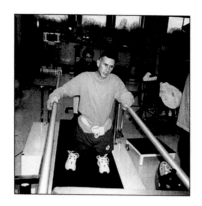

Just getting started

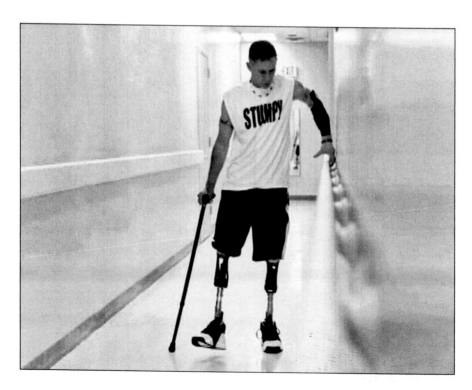

Test drive

Finally home

Together again with Kenny and Michael

Hitting the road on my Spyder

Woo hoo!

I'm taking over

At a Cubs game with Gary Sinise

people aren't comfortable with that. When I was a teenager, I never really opened up about myself much. I was more of a listener than a speaker. A lot of people used me as their sounding board. I always liked to think of myself as a sympathetic person, but I was a total pushover. I would sit and listen forever to anyone's and everyone's sob stories. Looking back, I suspect it was just easier for me to listen than it was to talk about myself.

A lot of things happened to change my outlook. My military training was part of it; it gave me the confidence to talk frankly and to the point. Unfortunately, I still didn't know much about getting other people to talk. The Army didn't seem interested in training me to help people get in touch with their feelings. As an MP, if I wanted information from a suspect, I knew how to beat it out of them. That's not a bad tactic in a war zone, but it's not much help when you're trying to figure out how to help a friend or colleague get through a divorce or cope with being laid off from work. Most people don't respond well to being told, "Stop crying or I'm gonna punch you in the throat."

Getting blown up was part of it, too. It certainly gave me an interesting story to tell. But the most important part of the equation, without a doubt, has been the traveling I've done.

In my younger days, even when I was in the Army, I never had many opportunities to visit different cities or countries. By the time I was discharged from the Army, I'd hardly been anywhere, and as a result I rarely met new people. That changed when I started working for Quantum Rehab. Thanks to my job as its national spokesperson, I travel almost all the time, and I'm always surrounded by new faces, which is great—I love meeting new people.

When you're surrounded by the same people every day, it's all so familiar. Even if something interesting happens, all the people know just as much about it as you do. That all changes when you meet someone new. They know nothing about you. You've had different experiences. As I traveled, it became easier to feel interesting and reveal my personality to strangers.

I was lucky in that after I finished rehab, I was able to talk about my pain in ways that advanced my career—first as part of the HBO documentary and then in news interviews and on *All My Children*. Not many people get paid to talk through their issues; I imagine even fewer get offered full-time jobs that encourage them to bare their soul as part of their duties. I know exactly how lucky I am for the opportunities that have come my way, and I realize that most people won't have access to these kinds of resources. But we can all find something that works for us. You just need to find the right audience.

Offering the obvious recommendations—go see a professional therapist, psychologist, psychiatrist, or a trusted member of the clergy—tends to rub some folks the wrong way. Maybe it's because going to these sorts of professionals for help feels like admitting defeat. If that's how you feel, I'd suggest you're looking at things wrong. Think of those folks as resources that are there to help you cope with the problems you face; as I've said before, use the tools you're given.

If the thought of sitting on a couch or in a confessional is just too much for you to take, though, it doesn't mean you don't have options. You can reach out to your family or your friends. After all, that's supposed to be what they're there for, right? No one else cares more about you or knows you so well as those who are closest to you, so in a lot of cases they're the best equipped to give you advice. Sometimes all you need to do is ask for it.

Maybe the problem you're dealing with is too personal to bring up with your nearest and dearest, though. Or maybe those people *are* the problem. What do you do then? Improvise. Go to a bar you've never visited before and never plan to set foot in again, and after a few rounds, spill your story to the bartender. Odds are, it won't be anything he or she hasn't heard before. If you don't drink, find a barber or a hairstylist and talk their ear off while they cut your hair. No hair? Go to a coffee shop and wait for some unsuspecting, sympathetic soul to make eye contact. Go to a support group, where the other people have been through the same shit you have, where they already understand what you're going through. You won't have to explain as much to them. They'll get you right away.

When you're coping with important situations, it's important that you talk to the right person and find the way that works best for you to get your feelings out into the open. This is part of the reason why people who work in gruesome jobs—such as soldiers, cops, firefighters, doctors, nurses, and EMTs—have reputations for indulging in gallows humor. When I was in Iraq, the other troops and I would crack jokes about everything, no matter how sick or twisted. That was just our way of coping with the stress of being in combat situations, day after day. We thought we were just being funny, but in hindsight I can see how badly we all needed to vent—to talk about what we were going through—and the only way we could do so was by making sick jokes.

If that works for you, go for it with my blessing. Sign up for open-mike night at your local comedy club and tell them Bryan Anderson sent you. You might not think your problems are so funny when you're neck-deep in them, but other people might. Hell, when all else fails, you can always talk to a dog. They never interrupt you, and they never betray your secrets. Now that I think about it, maybe we should all start with a dog.

The bottom line is if you really want to unburden yourself, there will always be a way, and I think you should do whatever you need to in order to find it. Why? Think of bad feelings as a can of beer that's been violently shaken. That's a lot of pressure built up inside something that can barely hold it. So what do you do when life leaves you all shook up? You have two choices. You can talk about whatever is bugging you—easing the can open and letting out the pressure one tiny bit at a time—or you can wait until life comes along and pops your top and you explode.

Your choice.

At first, the talking is just for you. Let that pressure out. You've got to do this before you can accept your situation and begin whatever healing—emotional, physical, or both—you need to do in order to move forward. But as you get better you can discover, like I did, that what you're going through can also be a tool to help someone else. Just think about that. Even when you're feeling a lot of hurt, when you're feeling helpless, you still have it in you to help someone else. It's true, although it might be hard to believe, for both you and the people around you.

Like I said, before the bombing, from when I was a teenager, I was used to people opening up to me. What always surprises me, though, is that there are people who know me but for whatever reason don't see me as someone who can give them advice or sympathy. Some people look at me and think that my life is worse off than theirs, or that I have more problems than they do—which is not necessarily true—and because of that they think that they shouldn't complain to me. When they're around me, they think they aren't allowed to feel bad about their problems just because I'm in a wheelchair. But this isn't true.

I'm as capable of helping people as I ever was, maybe even more than before, after what I've gone through. Not only does talking about things help me, helping others helps me, too. So talk to whoever you're comfortable with, and don't cut off anyone just because you think they're more tragic than you are. I don't want people to think that just because I'm in a wheelchair I *can't* help them with their problems. My disability isn't some kind of holier-than-thou badge of honor that makes my problems more important than anyone else's. I'm just a guy. If I want to help, let me. We're all in this together, right?

13

I'M NOT SPECIAL

It always makes me uncomfortable when someone describes me as a hero because I don't think of myself as one. The way I see it, I'm just another soldier who got hurt in Iraq. It's not as if I charged a machine-gunner's nest or jumped on top of a grenade. I was driving at five miles per hour on an empty street and got blown up. I don't call that bravery, I call that hitting the jackpot in the Iraqi Shit-Luck Sweepstakes. It could've happened to anyone.

And it *does* happen to anyone. Tens of thousands of U.S. and allied soldiers deployed in Iraq and Afghanistan have been hit by IEDs. Some of them were lucky enough to escape unhurt or with minor injuries, but most of them weren't. Lots of them were killed or maimed as I was. More than seventeen thousand veterans of the Iraq War have been sent home because they were wounded too severely to continue on active duty. If you want to applaud my service, I won't argue with you, but I want you to remember that my fellow veterans are heroes, too.

I've heard some folks say that we deserve to be honored not just because we were wounded but because it happened while we were serving our country in uniform during wartime. "Okay," I say, "but when a soldier gets hurt, what does it matter whether it happened in a war or during peacetime?" That usually gets people thinking for a few seconds.

Most often, the answer I get back is "It doesn't matter. If they were wounded while serving their country, it shouldn't matter where, when, or how."

That's a good answer, I think, because if you accept it as true, then you can say the same thing about police officers and firefighters who get hurt or killed in the line of duty. They wear uniforms and risk their lives for all of us every day. They're heroes, too, in my book.

So why revere soldiers, cops, and firefighters who get hurt in accidents but not civilians? After all, losing a leg hurts just as much whether you wear camouflage fatigues or faded blue jeans. What makes one person's injury heroic and the other one's ordinary? Is it just a matter of perception? Do we salute wounded soldiers, cops, and smoke jumpers simply because it makes a better story for the evening news? Does wearing a uniform make that much difference?

Yes, it does.

A uniform is more than just clothing. It's something that has to be earned. To wear one is to tell the world that you are part of something greater than yourself. The idea behind having a group of people wear a uniform is that they've put aside their individual personas—their wants, needs, and agendas—and taken on a shared identity. By wearing a uniform, a person becomes just one of many. This is the same reason that new recruits have their heads shaved when they first arrive at basic training. As much as possible, all the recruits are made to look the same, with identical haircuts, clothing, and boots. It sends a simple message: "You are not special. You are all equal. You are all in this together."

To wear a military, police, or firefighter's uniform is to accept risk. People who see you wearing one know immediately that you have pledged yourself to the service of others and willingly put yourself in danger. You're telling them that you are willing to give it all—to fight, kill, bleed, and die—to defend them, the way of life they enjoy, and the freedoms they cherish.

When you think about what it really means to wear that sort of uniform, you begin to understand that simply putting one on and going to work each day is an act of courage. That's what makes such persons' sacrifices and injuries in the line of duty inherently heroic. So when I say, "I'm not special," I don't mean that I think I'm not a good person. What I'm trying to say is that I'm just one of many. If I'm a hero, so are all the others like me.

For me, though, this raises an important question: Why don't we treat *all* our veterans like heroes? Why should some of them be given less credit or fewer rewards just because they were lucky enough to come home without serious physical injuries? Some soldiers who have never been wounded still suffer as a result of their combat experience. Many have memories that haunt them and psychological illnesses that go untreated for years because not enough people take posttraumatic stress disorders seriously. Why are there no parades for them? Why don't they get interviewed by HBO or photographed for the cover of *Esquire?*

Call me crazy, but I thought we were all in this *together.*

Don't misunderstand me. I'm not saying the government didn't do right by me, because it did. Army doctors saved my life, and I received the best care and rehabilitation at Walter Reed that anyone could ever hope for in my situation. On top of all that, shortly after I came home I was informed by the Army that I would be receiving a very generous, tax-free pension for the rest of my life. I have never felt that I was shortchanged or taken for granted by my country.

One of my favorite memories from my time at Walter Reed was the day that I received my payout from TSGLI, which is the Traumatic Servicemembers' Group Life Insurance fund. Basically, they pay onetime lump sums to soldiers like me who have lost limbs in combat action. The more you've left on the battlefield, the bigger a check they cut to you.

Well, I maxed out and got the whole enchilada—the maximum payout.

The day that money was wired into my bank account, my mom saw it first, because she had been taking care of my finances for me. When I came back from therapy that afternoon, she had a big smile on her face. "Come here," she said, beckoning me.

"What is it?"

"I pulled up your account," she said. "Y'know, just to check what was going on." She pointed at the screen of the laptop computer we'd been using, and I looked at it.

I saw all those zeroes, and my jaw dropped open against my chest.

"Oh my God," I said, like it was all one word. "Holy crap!"

That was a fun day—we went to the mall. We didn't go crazy or spend a lot of money, but it felt good to know that we could if we wanted to.

Money alone would not have been enough to get me through rehab, though. Cash is nice, but it doesn't hold your hand while you're learning to walk. It doesn't gently pat the sweat from your face while you lie awake all night, unable to sleep. Maybe you can use money to hire people to do these things, but you can't pay them to really care. That's why I thank God that I had my family with me when I woke up at Walter Reed.

Emotionally, my getting blown up hit my family much harder than it hit me. At the time I didn't understand why. Now I get it. All they'd ever wanted was the best for me, and they felt like there was nothing they could do to help me after I got hit. Of all of them, I think it was worst for my brother. Seeing what had happened to me really devastated Bobby. Of the two of us, he's always been more of a rebel and a troublemaker, and I've always been the good twin— the nice guy, the dependable one. So when he saw me lying in that hospital bed, it shook him up.

"It should've been me," he said to me once. "This doesn't make sense. It's not fair."

He kept asking me if there was anything he could do, but there wasn't. I didn't know how to make him understand that it was enough that he and the others were there—that their presence was all I needed. Just showing up was what mattered. Waking up surrounded by my family had made me realize that no matter what happened for the rest of my life, I would have them behind me. That's what really pushed me forward and kept me motivated during rehab: knowing that they were there, waiting for me to come out on the other side.

My mom showed me that by coming to live with me at Walter Reed. Just her being there would have made me feel better, even if she hadn't done anything (though, of course, she did everything and more). Having her with me made it possible for me to tell myself each day, *I'm gonna get through this, and it's gonna be all right.*

The truth is, no matter how many times I tell my story, I never feel like I give my mom enough credit.

Look around. Who's in *your* corner—helping you, encouraging you, just there for you? Your family? Your friends? Doctors, nurses, counselors? Whatever you do, don't take them for granted. It's easy to dump on these people. You can hold it together all day long, put a smile on your face for the rest of the world, and then come home and explode. You had a crap day at work but you can't yell at your boss, so you come home frustrated and angry and have no patience for your kids. You struggle with whatever it is you're struggling with but keep all your feelings bottled up inside because you don't want everyone to know your problems; you're sure they won't even care. Then you let it all out to the people closest to you. They see you at your worst: angry, crying, full of despair . . . and guess what? They're still there. And you know why? Because they care about you. They think you're special enough that they put up with all your crap.

So yeah, look around. Those are the people who make you special.

If anything in my life makes *me* feel special, it's my family. No medal, parade, twenty-one-gun salute, or anything else I can think of even comes close.

But as special as they make me feel, I really do think of myself as ordinary. However, sometimes people treat me as if I'm anything but.

Early in my rehab process, I was taken on a tour of the Pentagon. If you've never been there, let me tell you, that is an amazing place. If you've been there, you know what I'm talking about. My mom and I were with a group of other wounded vets from Walter Reed, and we all were led down this incredibly long main corridor. Lined up on either side of the hallway were all these people, military and civilians, who worked there. As we passed by, everyone had tears in their eyes as they clapped and cheered for us. I had never seen anything like it in my life. The raw emotion flooding that space was electric—I could feel it.

Near the end of the line, I met Secretary of Defense Donald Rumsfeld, who shook my hand and thanked me for my service. That blew my mind—me, a simple MP sergeant, shaking hands with the secretary of defense. It was like something out of a dream.

Then a general—whose name I'm ashamed to admit I can't remember—stepped out of an office into my path. I stopped my wheelchair, and the general looked me in the eye. "You like football, son?"

After nearly choking on my tongue, I stammered, "Yeah, of course I do."

"Wanna go to the Super Bowl?"

I blinked and stared at him, wide-eyed. "Sure."

He gave me, my mom, and my dad tickets to the Super Bowl in

Detroit. They were awesome seats, right on the fifty-yard line, down by the field. I got to watch the Steelers crush the Seahawks, 21–10 . . . when I wasn't watching the cheerleaders, that is.

Things like that still seem to happen to me from time to time. I don't seek them out, and I neither expect nor ask for special treatment from anyone. If there should come a day when I walk into your place of business, please feel free to say hi, but don't feel as if you need to treat me differently from any other customer. That said . . . on those rare occasions when someone goes out of their way to honor me for my service, I'm always surprised, flattered, and grateful.

Recently, as part of my renewed attempts to further my acting career, I decided to have my teeth straightened. After considering a number of different types of braces, the one that I liked best was called Invisalign. They seemed both convenient and inconspicuous, so I called a local dentist and made an appointment to come in for the preliminary consultation.

Long story short: they turned out to be a lot more expensive than I had expected. When I heard the price, I felt myself go pale. I think the dentist was afraid I'd pass out in her lobby. Still, even though they cost more than I had planned to spend, I decided they were worth it, and I told the dentist to go ahead and start the paperwork.

A few weeks later I returned to her office so she could take some impressions that would be used to create the first plastic aligner for my teeth. When she was finished, I went back to the lobby to pay the receptionist for that day's visit. As my credit card was being processed, the dentist came out to the lobby. She was smiling at me.

I asked, "What's going on?"

"I thought you might like to know that's the last payment you'll have to make for your Invisalign," she said. "I'm only going to charge you for the initial visit and the impression set we made today. The rest of your treatment is on me, as a thank you for your service."

She'd caught me totally off guard. I didn't know what to say, so I mumbled, "Thanks."

"Our pleasure."

Favors such as those make me happy—not because I'm getting something free or at a discount but because it's proof that some of my fellow citizens still care about their men and women in uniform, still honor our sacrifices, and want to do something, *anything*, to give a bit of themselves for us. No one who puts on the uniform of an armed service expects to be praised or rewarded simply for doing their job—all any of us really ask in return, I think, is respect. But when the people we've served make an effort to express their gratitude, that's a better reward than anything else I can imagine. And it really isn't about the dollar value, it's about the gesture.

Nothing beats the outpouring of support my family received for my homecoming, though.

While I was in rehab, my family and neighbors helped remodel my parents' house. My uncle Rick and friend Rod Blain persuaded the community to pitch in. Contractors donated materials and supplies, and ordinary folks donated their time, money, and labor. Understand that this wasn't just a simple upgrade to make it wheelchair accessible for me; it was more than a few ramps and some railings. What they really did was gut my family's house and build a new one from the inside out. I think the only parts they left intact were the front wall, the roof, and the living room. Everything else is brand-new and completely different.

All told, it was a roughly $400,000 renovation. This is the kind of everyday miracle that can happen when good people choose to take action.

I also put more than half my TSGLI payment toward that renovation, because I considered it an investment in my future, and because it was a way to thank my family for being there for me when I'd needed them most.

Next, I invested more than half of what I had left to open an IRA, into which I still deposit a chunk of my monthly service pension, because I want to retire in style when I get old.

Then I bought a fourteen-foot jet boat. Because being responsible is good, but what's the point unless you remember to have a little fun once in a while, right?

So much has been given to me, and I truly appreciate it. But what really makes my life full is being able to give back to others. Not only do I get great joy and a sense of purpose when I can help someone, it also affirms for me that I'm whole enough—that I have enough—to give to someone else. I think giving and helping others is crucial to healing. Being able to reach out to others means you're not focused solely on yourself. You can put aside your own troubles, even for just a while, and look outward to see who else needs help. And by serving others, you're showing others, and more important, yourself, that you have worth and have something to give.

Something that is very important to me and that I give a lot to is advocacy for veterans. I'm pleased and humbled that so many people I've met have thanked me for my service and praised me for the sacrifices I made while in uniform. I still wish, however, that we did more as a country to serve and honor our veterans, who have done and given so much for all of us. It often seems that we set aside only two days of each year—Memorial Day and Veterans Day—to pay tribute to our men and women in uniform; I think we need to remember them *every* day. I try to do my share. I think the stuff I'm doing makes people aware of what a lot of veterans are going through, and when people really know what's going on, they're more likely to chip in and help. My work as a spokesperson with USA Cares is like that. USA Cares gives financial aid to post-9/11 military personnel and their families. The bills can pile up while someone is serving, and the transition back to civilian life can be hard. USA Cares keeps veterans out of the red until they get back on their feet.

Too many veterans come home after serving in combat—sometimes multiple tours—to find themselves out of step with the country they left behind. It can be disorienting to return to civilian life after a long time in the service. It's even more difficult for disabled veterans, especially those who have lost limbs, been paralyzed, or suffered a traumatic brain injury. So much happens so quickly to a veteran after arriving at Walter Reed that it can be confusing, to say the least. It's as if one day you're thousands of miles from home, in the thick of combat, and the next day you wake up in Washington, D.C., missing parts of yourself and wondering how you landed in the middle of a paperwork blizzard.

One place we might start would be to provide better financial counseling to returning veterans, especially those who are due to receive generous pensions and large payouts from TSGLI. Let me say from experience, when you're fighting to relearn how to walk after having half your body blown away, it's not a good time to be making financial decisions by yourself.

During the rehab period, when many wounded veterans are struggling to regain mobility or adapt to prosthetic limbs, the government buries them in red tape at the same time as it drops a ton of money and benefits into their laps. I was lucky because I had my mom there with me at Walter Reed to shield me from the bureaucratic bullshit and keep track of my finances. Not all my fellow soldiers were so lucky. Most of the soldiers I knew at Walter Reed, when they got their TSGLI checks, ran out and blew all their money on cars, quads, or motorcycles. Some of them bought televisions so big that they didn't fit in their shoe-box-size hotel rooms.

I watched them, shook my head, and said, "All right. Now you've spent all your money. How's that gonna help you? Sure, you've got a car free and clear without a note, but how are you gonna be able to afford to go back to real life?" It's as if they just weren't thinking ahead.

Those are the sorts of dumb mistakes that can be avoided with a bit of education.

This, among other reasons, is why I've started spending time on Capitol Hill in Washington, meeting and getting to know different members of Congress. The wounds I suffered in Iraq and the notoriety they brought me after I came home helped me get a job at Quantum Rehab. The people I've met while working at Quantum have introduced me to several elected officials in our national government. I use these connections to serve as an advocate for veterans and the disabled.

There is a lot more we could do to improve the quality of life for members of both groups—especially for those individuals who happen to belong to both of them. We need better funding for the Veterans Administration, more full scholarships for veterans, better-staffed facilities and more up-to-date medical equipment for wounded soldiers, tax relief for disabled veterans who were wounded while on active duty, and better coverage for all disabled Americans who rely upon Medicare and Medicaid for such necessities as power wheelchairs so that they can lead fuller lives outside their homes, as active members of society.

I'm just one person, and I can't make these changes happen by myself. It's my hope that if I lead the way, more concerned citizens will join me in writing to their elected representatives to voice their support for these important changes to our national spending priorities.

If you can help me bring about that kind of change, you'll all be *my* heroes.

14

SEVEN STORIES

One of my favorite pastimes when I'm traveling and meeting new people is telling them my stories and then listening to theirs. I get to hear some pretty wild stuff from all kinds of people across the country, believe me. So since we've gone through a lot of the heavy shit in my life, it's time to lighten things up and tell some funny stories. I think there are certain people who expect me to tell only the grim stuff, but like I've said, I don't like to have my life defined by my injuries. Neither should you. Even if something horrible has happened to you, it doesn't mean the rest of your life will never be fun again. In that spirit, I'm going to tell you a few short stories just because they're fun—and they all happened after I got blown up.

Two things you should know before reading further: a few names have been changed to protect the guilty. And if, by some chance, you happen to learn something or take some measure of inspiration from one of these . . . you've probably read it wrong.

―――――――――

Most soldiers who go through rehab at Walter Reed, when they're done with therapy each day, can do whatever they want. Being soldiers, the majority of them tend to drink a lot. They go to the bars pretty much every day, and then they're hungover the next morning. "Bad hangover" is the number one excuse for missed therapy sessions at Walter Reed.

During my rehab, I watched all this nonsense from a distance and suspected it was the reason why so many soldiers needed to stay at Walter Reed as long as they did. I didn't want to slow down my recovery that way, so I didn't go out very often. In fact, I hardly left the base at all during the thirteen months I lived there. The one night I really wanted to go out, however, was the Friday of Memorial Day weekend. Most of the soldiers' family members had left to spend the long weekend at home, and my folks were among them.

That left me with plenty of free time to hang out with my buddy Nick. He was a Marine whose wounds in Iraq had made him an above-the-knee bilateral amputee. Unlike me, he still had both his arms, but because we both had lost our legs above the knees, we had very similar rehab regimens, and that meant we spent a lot of time together. It was good to have someone I could talk to who really understood what I was going through. We bonded over that.

When Nick and I heard that the regular crew of bar hoppers and pub crawlers were planning a big night out on Friday, we knew we wanted in. We tracked down a few of those guys and told them we wanted to join them Friday night. They seemed excited to have us along, and we all agreed to meet at six-thirty in the lobby of the Malone House, where I lived.

Most of the soldiers skipped therapy that Friday, but Nick and I went to all our sessions, as usual. When we finally finished, we were running late. I hurried back to the Malone House to clean up and change my clothes. I made it back downstairs to the lobby about twenty minutes late. Nick was the only one there. He had arrived fifteen minutes late to find the lobby empty.

"They left us," he said. "Those fuckin' jerks couldn't even wait fifteen minutes."

"Are you kidding me?" I couldn't believe it. I was so pissed off. "We told them we wanted to go with them! They said they'd give us rides!"

Nick shrugged. "Yeah, well, they lied."

I spent a few seconds cursing, then I asked him, "What do you want to do now?"

"I don't know about you, but I still want to go out."

"So do I."

"Okay, then let's make it happen."

We left the lobby and went looking for a ride into the city.

Part of what made this situation such a hassle was that taxi service in the Washington, D.C., area really sucks. If we had called for a cab, it would have taken at least ninety minutes just for one to get to Walter Reed and meet us at the security checkpoint. The flip side of this problem was that once we were in the city, the chances of us finding a taxi that would have been willing to take us back to Walter Reed were close to nil. Most cabdrivers hate driving out to Walter

Reed because it's an Army base. To get through the checkpoint and drive onto the base, a visitor needs to show credentials and have their name logged into the system; for some reason, cabbies hate that with a passion. That's why we didn't bother calling a cab; we thought that finding someone to give us a ride out and back would be quicker and easier.

We thought wrong. By seven o'clock, pretty much anyone we might have begged a ride from had already left the base. Things were looking bleak. Then, just as Nick and I were getting ready to resign ourselves to a night of microwave popcorn and movies on DVD, I noticed that my mom had left her rental car in front of the Malone House. I thought she had driven it to the airport for her trip home, but apparently she had taken a cab. I assume she had reasoned that the rental car would be safer on an Army base than in an airport's short-term parking lot.

I pointed at the rental car and looked at Nick. "There's our ride! What do you think?"

"Who'll drive it?"

"We will. How hard can it be?"

He thought about this for a few seconds. "Worth a shot. Go get the keys."

I went back to my room, grabbed the keys, came back, and opened the car. Nick and I crawled in through the rear doors and pulled our chairs in behind us. I climbed forward into the driver's seat. Nick crawled down by the pedals. I stuck the key in the ignition. "Ready?"

"Absolutely."

"All right, man. You know this is gonna take a lot of communication, right?"

"No problem. We're five-by-five."

"We'll need to come up with some kind of system."

"Fuck it. Let's just back out of the parking spot and see how it goes."

"Brake," I said.

"Check."

I put the car in reverse and looked over my shoulder. "We're clear. Ease off the brake. Just a tap on the gas. A little more . . . easy . . ." The car inched backward, and I guided it through a slow turn, out of the spot. "All right. A little bit more. Okay, slow down. Slower. Brake. Stop!" Nick pushed hard on the brake pedal, and the tires screeched as the car lurched to a halt. "Nice." I shifted into drive. "Okay, ease off the brake. Give it a little gas . . . a bit more . . . slowly . . ."

We came up with our own vocabulary. "Go" meant "Gradually increase the gas." "Hit it" was code for "Hit the gas hard, now!" "Slow" was how I told Nick to gradually slow down. Sometimes it was as simple as saying, "Okay, a little harder, a little harder . . . a little softer . . . now harder . . . STOP!" Imagine if you had to give your legs and feet specific verbal instructions for every little thing you do while driving. That's what it was like. In traffic.

Ten minutes later, we arrived at the bar.

We even parallel-parked, because I'm *that* good.

Nick and I crawled into the backseat, unloaded our wheelchairs, climbed out of the car into them, and locked the car behind us. As we rolled into the bar, the jerks who had left us behind looked up, saw us, and shouted, "Hey! You made it!"

Nick grumbled under his breath, "No thanks to you."

One of the other guys asked, "How'd you get here?"

"You don't want to know," I said.

Nick added, "Don't worry about it."

Once Nick got over being pissed off, we had a good time. We had a few beers, and soon we were feeling pretty good. We knew we didn't want to stay until the bar closed, because the police stake out the bars at last call on holiday weekends, looking for drunk drivers, and I didn't want a cop to see two dudes with no legs crawling into a car's driver's seat. Nick and I left the bar around midnight to beat the crowd. Outside, everything was quiet. It was early and the weather was gorgeous, so we didn't hit much traffic on the ride home to Walter Reed.

Despite our weird arrangement, it was a nice drive. We even got to use the cruise control for a while. Everything went great right until the moment when I pulled up to Walter Reed.

That was when I remembered we had to drive back *onto an Army base.*

If you've never been to a military base before, let me explain. To be admitted to a U.S. military facility, visitors need to show valid identification—a driver's license, military ID card, passport, whatever—to the guards at the security checkpoint. Regulations require the guards to verify the identity of each person in every vehicle and permit only authorized visitors to enter.

As Nick and I pulled up the driveway, and I saw the bright lights of the gate to the Walter Reed campus, I muttered, "Oh, shit." I was sure we were screwed, but I played it cool for Nick. "Chill out," I whispered. "I've got this. Keep your head down, and stay quiet. We'll be okay."

I pulled up and stopped. The guard stepped out of his hut and approached my car. I took out my military ID card with two fingers, handed it casually out the open window, and avoided eye contact with the guard as I offered it to him.

He didn't take my card or even look at me. Instead, he pointed to the side of the road. "Pull forward for random inspection, please."

I froze for half a second, and then I put away my ID and shifted the car into gear. As I pulled over and parked it, I mumbled to Nick, "So, dude . . . ready to go to jail?"

Nick was surprisingly calm about the whole thing. "Fuck, man, what're they gonna do? Look at us. Can they possibly make our shit any worse than it already is?"

"Dude, if I've learned anything in the Army, it's that shit can *always* be worse."

I parked the car, popped the hood, and opened the trunk, but I was careful not to open any of the doors. The guard walked up, circled the car, and said, "Would you mind stepping out of the vehicle, sir?" Then he opened the door for me.

Or, should I say, for us.

Nick and I stared up at the guard with what I can only imagine were the two dumbest, most stunned-stupid expressions in all of history. I'm pretty sure I actually said, "Duh . . ."

The guard looked back at us, frozen just like we were. He didn't say anything for close to half a minute—not a single word. Nick and I knew we were in some seriously deep shit, so we kept our mouths shut.

Finally, the guard blinked, shook his head, looked around, and said, "Shit, man, you guys made it this far . . . Just go. Just . . . *go.*" He shut my door and waved us through the gate.

"Hell, yeah," I said. "Hit it, Nick." He pressed on the gas and we took off.

Ever since then, I've wondered what must have been going through that guard's mind. Imagine being that soldier working the gate at Walter Reed at half-past midnight, the only person on duty at that post, when you discover two disabled soldiers—two guys who were both blown to shit in Iraq—working as a team to drive the same car. We both had valid driver's licenses. How would you even call that in?

"Um, dispatch? I've got two guys with zero legs driving one car. Please advise."

I used to be an MP, and even I don't know what the charge would be. Driving without legs? I can see some prosecutor paging frantically through the criminal code and coming up empty. "Well, it doesn't say the driver must actually have legs. Or be in control of the pedals."

Call me crazy, but I bet that would make a great plot twist on an episode of *Law & Order.*

————————

This next story isn't funny, but it is pretty amazing, so I've just gotta tell you about it. When Mark Kirk, who's now a senator for Illinois, was still a representative, he invited me and my friend Timmy to President George W. Bush's 2007 State of the Union address. He also wanted me to help with passing a bill to raise money for a disabled veterans' memorial on Capitol Hill. The bill was called the American Veterans Disabled for Life Commemorative Coin Act. The idea was that there would be a special one-dollar coin minted to honor veterans who had been disabled in the line of duty, and it would be sold for eleven dollars, with the extra ten dollars for building the memorial.

He took me around to different congressmen to try to get them to back the bill. I would just tell my story and explain why I thought disabled veterans deserved a memorial. During a meeting, one of the congressmen got up and left, right while I was talking. I wondered what that was about, but then I figured, *Hey, these are busy people.* After about five minutes, he came back and said he'd support the bill. He was kind of a heavy hitter on Capitol Hill, so once he declared he was backing the bill, a lot of other people jumped on board, too.

It took a while, but eventually, the bill passed both houses of Congress and the coins came out early in 2010. Later on, Kirk told me that the reason the congressman had left the meeting was that he'd been so moved by my story that he'd teared up, and that kind of sealed the deal with that guy. So Kirk said the bill got passed basically because of me and Gary Sinise, who's the spokesperson for the American Veterans Disabled for Life Memorial.

I felt proud that I'd been able to help accomplish something really important. It helped me understand that even after we've been knocked down by the worst that life can do to us, we can recover and still do things that are important to us, and enjoy the ride while we're doing it.

And sometimes, it's precisely *because* you've been through something terrible that you later get the chance to do something wonderful. Our lives will be what we make of them.

Later that spring, I got a call from Luzerne County Community College in Pennsylvania, asking if I would be their commencement speaker. I said, "Sure," even though I didn't really know what I was getting myself into. I'd never given a speech and didn't think of myself as a speaker, but I'm always up for a challenge. Besides, I'd talked to congressmen, so I figured I had some experience. I'd just started working with Pride Mobility, and Dick said, "We'll have the speech written up for you."

I thought, *Okay, great, I'm all set.* They sent the speech to me a couple days before I was supposed to give it. While I was on the plane out to Pennsylvania, I looked through the speech more closely. I started crossing out whole paragraphs: *Nope, I'm not saying this.* I started writing key phrases of points I wanted to hit. The original speech had a lot of good points, but they just weren't written the way I would say them. I revised everything and got it down to what I wanted to say. Everything seemed under control.

Then came the day of graduation. I was at the venue, I had my prosthetic legs on, and I'd been given a gown and a sash, the whole works. The ceremony was in the Wachovia Arena, and as all the graduates started coming in, it finally hit me that there was a few thousand people there. I looked around, saw a JumboTron hanging in the middle of the arena, and realized there were video cameras. This thing was a whole lot bigger than I had imagined and seemed to be getting bigger every second. Then I heard them call my name.

I stood up, and I was kind of freaking out. That's when I looked out across the arena and saw myself on the JumboTron. *Holy shit!* I stared across the sea of people as I walked across the stage. It felt like I wasn't blinking. I stopped at the podium, looked down at my speech, and thought, *I don't want to do this.*

But then my Army training kicked in. I had agreed to do this, so I was going to do it. That's how it had been for me in the Army. After a couple years in, I didn't want to be in the Army anymore.

I knew I wasn't going to do that for the rest of my life, but I'd made the commitment and I was going to honor it. There were things in Iraq that I didn't want to do, but I just had to.

Standing at the podium, I knew this was just one of those times. I told myself, *You have to do it.*

I looked down at my speech again, and I realized that everything I'd written down, I didn't want to say anymore. *Shit. Shit!* I turned the pages facedown, looked up . . . and I just started talking.

"You guys have accomplished something that not everybody does," I said, "and now it's the next step. But your work's not over yet; success isn't just going to come to you. You still have to go out and find jobs, and do what you want to do. You have to go out into the world and live."

I talked for ten or fifteen minutes and that was it. I got away from that podium. What a relief.

Afterward, members of the faculty came up to me and said, "That was amazing, that was the best speech we've had in thirty years." So, that's how I got started doing public speaking, and I got an honorary doctorate out of it. I'm a doctor of public service, if you can believe that.

Giving that speech by the seat of my pants turned out to be one of the best things I've ever done. If I'd really thought about it beforehand, or known how overwhelming it was going to feel, I might not have gone through with it, but I'm so glad I did. It's just another example of how good it is to stretch yourself out of your comfort zone. You'll never *experience* something new if you don't *try* something new. It sounds obvious, I know, but just think about how many times you've shrugged your shoulders at something you've never tried before and decided not to do it for no other reason than that. You really don't know what you're missing, and it may be something really cool.

When *Alive Day Memories* was done, HBO flew five of us guys that had been in the documentary out to Beverly Hills for the premiere. We all went to a big HBO party, and it seemed as if everyone who was on HBO was there. I saw all kinds of actors, including the casts of *Entourage, Curb Your Enthusiasm*, and *John from Cincinnati*. The place that hosted the party was amazing. There was a pool that had spouts of fire coming up out of it. I'm not sure why you'd want flames shooting out of a pool, but somehow it fit in with California and celebrities.

I had my prosthetic legs on, so I left my chair parked in a corner somewhere and walked around. I saw a bunch of the guys from *Entourage* standing together: Kevin Connolly, Kevin Dillon, Adrian Grenier, and Jerry Ferrara. I went up and introduced myself, and they were all really cool. Me and the two Kevins and Brian Van Holt, one of the guys from *John from Cincinnati*, ended up hanging out together through the whole party. The rest of the *Entourage* group left early.

We were all sitting together when we saw James Gandolfini come in. All the actors started talking about Jim and how awesome he is. There was just something about the way they talked, I finally looked at them and said, "Wait, you guys don't know Jim?" It turned out the *Entourage* guys had never met him. So I told them about working with him on the documentary and how he was just a big teddy bear.

Then I said, "Hold on. Let *me* introduce you." I got up and walked over to Jim and said, "Hey, I got some people who want to meet you." So I brought him over and introduced him to the *Entourage* people, which was awesome.

Later on the two Kevins and me were sitting by the pool, and they said, "We'll give you a thousand dollars if you push Jim into the pool."

I said, "Really?"—kind of sarcastically, not believing them. Just then Jim walked by, so I stood up and put my hands on him. I said, "I just got offered a thousand bucks to push you into this pool."

He looked at me, looked at his drink, then said, "Let me have another drink, and then I'll split the money with you." We laughed and left it at that.

When that party ended, we didn't want to stop, so we headed over to the club in the hotel next door for an afterparty. I didn't want to walk anymore, so I'd taken off my legs and jumped into my wheelchair. Jim pointed at my legs and said, "Let me get those." He grabbed them and started walking along, carrying one in each hand. As Jim, the two Kevins, and me and my friends Timmy and Eliot headed toward the club, this woman came down the sidewalk and passed in front of us, but didn't notice who any of us were. Jim looked back at us with a shit-eating grin—then he ran up to her and started kicking her in the ass with my legs.

She kind of freaked out and turned around: "What the hell?!" Then she saw it was James Gandolfini and was like, "Holy shit, Tony Soprano!"

He likes doing crazy stuff like that. At the Washington, D.C., premiere, he said he needed to smoke a stogey, so I went with him to have a cigarette. Five of us ended up out there. Jim looked around at all of us and said, "I'll be right back." He went into the hotel lobby and started dragging out two big cushy chairs. So a couple of the other guys went and got some more and we sat out there on a street corner in D.C. smoking and drinking until some hotel employees came out and busted us.

Some people just don't know how to have fun, I guess.

Anyway, back to Beverly Hills.

Later that night, we were in a back room of the club at the hotel, and Kevin Dillon said, "Hey, we should all do shots of Patrón, bro!" Everyone agreed, so he got the waiter and had them bring over the shots. Then he jumped up, grabbed one of my legs, and ran away with it.

I sat there and thought, *All right. Kevin Dillon just stole one of my legs.* When he finally came back with it, he had filled it with beer, and he passed it around and we all drank out of it.

What can I say? That Kevin Dillon is a classy guy.

———————

So much stuff happened to me after I appeared on the cover of *Esquire* that I can still hardly believe it. In the article, I'd said I wanted to be a stuntman and an actor, so after it came out I got a call from a guy named Douglas Crosby. He was a stunt coordinator, and he said he was working on a new Mickey Rourke movie, *The Wrestler.* Douglas wanted to give me a shot to see if I'd be able to do the job. He's a great guy who likes to give people in bad situations a chance to break out of them. He asked me to come to South Philadelphia, where they were shooting some scenes for the movie at the Alhambra Arena. He brought me out there for two days in February 2008. We worked from four in the afternoon until four in the morning both days.

It was a scene in which Mickey's character, Randy "The Ram" Robinson, is wrestling at this semi-underground event called Combat Zone Wrestling, or CZW, and they do crazy stuff. They call it "ultraviolent wrestling." This wasn't all staged for the movie; this was one of CZW's regular events. We were there filming before, during, and a little bit after the real deal. When we got there, Douglas brought me up to meet Mickey Rourke and Darren Aronofsky, the director. And Mickey was like, "He's a soldier? All right, cool. You know what? I got you now, you're with me, you're taken care of, that's it." And he kind of took me under his wing for the couple of days that I was there.

Then we sat around talking about what we could do to work me into the movie. We spitballed a few ideas. In the scene, Randy the Ram was supposed to hit the other wrestler with a folding chair—a classic wrestling move, right? I think it was Douglas who said, "Do those legs come off? Can we hit somebody with one?" He knew my personality, knew that I'd want to do something crazy.

I was like, "Yeah!" So we decided to use one of my legs instead of the folding chair. I'd be one of the people in the audience, and I'd give Randy the Ram one of my legs. At first, Darren Aronofsky was worried we'd break it, but I told him they're made out of high-tech material, that there was no way they'd break. Then he asked Mickey what he thought, and Mickey said, "Let's go for it."

That was it, we just talked about it, and then we started shooting in front of the real crowd that was there for CZW. When I offered my leg to Randy the Ram, the crowd started chanting, "Use the leg! Use the leg!" It was really cool to see how it was done. We shot it like three or four different times.

When we weren't shooting, I'd sit off to the side of the set, and

Mickey and I would bullshit with each other. He asked me about what had happened to me, so I told him all about that. We didn't get to spend a lot of time together since I was there for only a couple of days. But I can't thank Douglas enough for that experience. It showed me that there really are people out there willing to help and give others a chance at doing something new.

Later that year, in December, I was invited out to Los Angeles for the movie's premiere, where I actually got to walk the red carpet next to Mickey. Marisa Tomei was at the premiere, of course. I hadn't gotten to meet her during filming because she wasn't part of the scenes I was in, so she wasn't there. So, at the premiere I told Mickey, "Hey, I want to meet Marisa Tomei. Can you introduce me?"

He said, "Sure. We'll go find her after the show."

Then, just as I was sitting down before the show, Marisa Tomei was standing in the aisle, barely three feet from me. I was sitting with Randy "The Natural" Couture and Gina "Crush" Carano—there were all kinds of wrestlers and extreme fighters there. It was cool to be sitting with them, but there was Marisa! She was talking to somebody, and I really wanted to just reach over and tap her on the arm, and say, "Hey, I'm Bryan Anderson, I just wanted to say, 'Hi, I think you're awesome.' " But I didn't, because I thought, Mickey and I will go find her afterward, and I don't want to interrupt her.

After the show, Mickey and I searched the whole theater for her, but the place was packed, and we couldn't find her. I don't know, maybe she had left. He was bummed about it, maybe even more than I was; he'd really wanted to introduce me to her.

Maybe it just wasn't meant to be. Or maybe it's meant to be at a different time. That's how I try to deal with everything: If it's supposed to happen, it happens, so no need to worry about it.

Besides, how can I complain? I got to hang with Mickey Rourke!

I mentioned earlier that I once dated a girl who worked at one of our dealers' stores. Our first date really was a wild ride, and you need to hear the whole story. I've done a lot of trips for Pride Mobility, but back in the summer of 2008 it was my first road trip for them. I was going with Dick and Dan Pickett, one of our corporate representatives. We went down to Knoxville, Tennessee, to visit one of our dealers, do a meet-and-greet, and record some media spots. After we had finished with all the official stuff, Dick and I invited the dealership owner and some of the employees out to dinner. Among them was a young woman, Casey, and she was really nice.

We all had a good dinner, and afterward I asked Casey and another employee, Jessica, if they wanted to come back to my hotel to talk some more and just hang out for a while. They said yes.

So, we all went back to the hotel, part of a low-budget chain, somewhere in Knoxville. It was the kind of place where there were two floors, all the doors opened to the outside, and the second floor was ringed by a balcony. When I checked in, I had asked if they had any smoking rooms. The clerk said, "Yeah, but they're on the second floor."

I said, "That's fine."

"But we don't have an elevator."

"Oh."

"But we have a ramp."

"Oh, okay. As long as you've got a ramp, I'm good." They checked me in, and I went to find my room. I rolled down to the "ramp," and it was literally a cemented-over flight of stairs with a landing. It was an enclosed stairwell with no railings, and this thing was steep as hell.

The problem was that a flight of stairs is much steeper than a ramp. Stairs are like a thirty- to forty-degree angle, but ramps for wheelchairs should be no more than five to ten degrees. That's a huge difference. Stairs are fine when you're walking up them, but imagine putting a piece of plywood on your stairs and then trying to push a wheelchair up that slope. I couldn't push myself up that incline now, let alone when I was first getting used to a manual wheelchair.

Dick had somehow gotten me up and down the thing before dinner, but after dinner I had to face it with these two young women. The two of them struggled together, with me helping as much as I could, and were able to push me up. Miraculously, we got back to my room. We listened to music, had a good time, did some dancing, and knocked back a few drinks. Casey and I both smoked, and by around two in the morning, we were out of cigarettes. Earlier that day I had bought cigarettes, but they were in the van that Dick, Dan, and I had been driving around in. And Dick and Dan had the keys.

Casey and I looked at each other, knowing we desperately needed cigarettes. I said, "Well, Dick and Dan said if I needed anything—*anything at all*—to knock on their door. And all we need are the keys." This trip was the first time I'd met Dan, and only the second or third time I'd hung around with Dick. I didn't know either of these guys that well, and it was two thirty in the morning.

"Fuck it," I said to Casey. "Let's go wake 'em up."

The real problem was that Dick and Dan were down on the first floor. Meaning the ramp from hell was between us and the keys. I asked Casey, "Will you help me down the ramp?"

She said, "Oh, yeah, absolutely."

Casey was wearing a tank top and shorts and she'd taken off her shoes, but was still wearing her socks. Not exactly dressed for hauling a guy up and down that ramp. But we rolled out there, and I said, "All right, have you got me?"

She grabbed the handles of the chair, locked her knees, and pushed me slowly to the edge. But as soon as I got on that steep slope, I started flying down. Casey was still holding on, stiff-legged, shrieking, "Ohmygod, ohmygod, ohmygod!" The concrete ramp was painted, and her socks were just sliding, as if she were skiing down a mountain. We zoomed down to the landing and then right across toward the far wall. Casey was still right behind me. When the chair hit the wall, I flew forward, smacked into the wall, and bounced back into my chair. It was like an insane amusement park ride. Casey didn't make a sound, but then I started laughing, so she started laughing. I was okay and still thinking of cigarettes.

I looked back at her and said, "Just one more to go. You ready?" What else were we going to do? We were already halfway down the death ramp. She said she was good to go, so we turned around and moved up to the edge of the next one. Casey did the same thing, just held on tight and locked her knees, and off we went, shooting down the ramp with her screaming, "Ohmygod, ohmygod, ohm-ygod!"

But when Casey hit the sidewalk, where it wasn't painted, her socks got traction, and she came to a dead halt. She let go of the chair—but I kept going, because there wasn't a wall in front of me this time, just a parking block at the edge of the sidewalk. When the chair hit that, my body went ballistic and just flew. I landed on the ground, rolling around and laughing.

Casey was freaked for a moment, but I was like, "Okay, we survived!" That's what counts, in my opinion. Sure, I'd flown like an Angry Bird before I crashed, but I was all right. Enjoy the moment, enjoy all that you can, that's what I say.

So, we finally got to Dick and Dan's room, and through the door I heard them both sawing logs, loud as can be, sound asleep. I looked up at Casey, then back at the door. I shook my head, feeling a bit sorry for those guys, but then I knocked on the door. I heard one of them stop snoring, get up, and plod over to look through the peephole.

Dan swung the door open and glared down at me with this *what-the-fuck-do-you-want* look, and I stared back at him and said, feeling kind of guilty, "I need the keys to the van." He looked over his shoulder at the clock, then back at me, still with that homicidal scowl on his face. I thought he was going to tell me what to do with the keys—but then he noticed Casey standing behind me. He gave her a once-over . . . and then he smiled at me. "No problem," he said, and he handed over the keys.

Moral of the story: If you're going to wake a guy up at two in the morning just to get cigarettes out of his van, it doesn't hurt to have a beautiful woman by your side.

Rolling Meadows and Arlington Heights put on a festival called "Frontier Days" every Fourth of July weekend. It's a great chance to meet up with friends I don't see very often, because everyone goes and I'm always bumping into people. When I went in 2009, I ran into one of my high-school friends, Becky Vigna. We talked for a while, and she invited me over to her house, which was just down the street from my condo, to hang out and go swimming or whatever. One of her sisters, Lindsay, was there, too, and I thought she was amazing, but I was feeling a little shy.

Later that summer I went over to Becky's house on my Can-Am Spyder, which is a three-wheeled motorcycle. I rolled up and Becky and all three of her sisters were tanning in the driveway, all looking great. And I was thinking, *How did I get this lucky?*

So I hung out and talked with Becky and Lindsay a bit more. I asked Lindsay if she wanted to go for a ride on my bike. She did. While we were out riding, I asked if she wanted to go to a concert with me. I was going to see the Lt. Dan Band, Gary Sinise's band, out in Wheaton. She said yes.

The night of the concert, I picked her up and drove out to Wheaton. Since I'm friends with Gary, we got to use private parking in the back, where the band parked. Once we got inside, we were led to a cordoned-off space in front of the stage, an area about twenty feet deep between the stage and the front row designed to keep the crowd back for security reasons, and we got to watch the show from there.

The whole concert was awsome. Right away, Gary started giving me looks, pointing at me, giving me the thumbs-up—you know, indicating that the girl I was with was fine. During one song, he came down the steps off the stage, while he was playing, and walked over to me. When there was a break in the song he reached out his hand so I could give him a high five, then he went over to Lindsay, shook her hand, and gave me another approving look. Then he went back up onstage. I thought that was so cool, that he would take the time for me like that, right in the middle of a show.

After the concert, the band had a meet-and-greet, and there was a whole line of people waiting for photo ops with Gary and the guys. Lindsay sat on my lap while I zoomed along in my power wheelchair to the front of the line, and I knocked on the door. The security guys let me in, and I introduced Gary to Lindsay. I was sure it was the best first date ever.

On the way home, I looked at Lindsay and said, "You know, I like you. I like you a lot." I was kind of nervous. "Do you want to start dating or whatever?"

She said, "Yes." That's how it all started, and she was fantastic.

But I soon learned there's one problem with having the perfect first date. You spend the rest of the relationship haunted by the question, *How the hell can I ever top that?*

I never did. But damn, it was awesome while it lasted.

Okay, I know I said you shouldn't learn anything or be inspired by my funny stories, but I was wrong. Sure, sometimes all you really want is an entertaining story and nothing else, like a blockbuster summer movie. But I think these stories are also hopeful stories. You don't have to continuously live in the moment of whatever tragedy has hammered down on you. You will get out from under that shadow. But there's something else that will help you leave that shadow behind, and it's not so obvious. Just like I don't want to stand around telling stories about getting blown up all the time, I also don't want to always tell funny stories from before I went to Iraq. As good as some of them are, I'm not about remembering only the glory days; I want to focus on new experiences. My life didn't end in Iraq, it just changed. I've got lots to look forward to, and you do, too. Someday, I hope to hear your funny stories.

15

IT'S ALL ABOUT HAVING FUN

If I have what one would call a philosophy of life, this is it: it's all about having fun.

I know that might not sound like a very deep motto, but there's more to it than goofing off. Part of having fun is doing so responsibly. Don't spend time entertaining yourself when you have work to do. Keeping your word and meeting your obligations should always come first—but those things shouldn't take up every minute of your life. It's vital that you make some time in your life for having fun. What I'm talking about is *enjoying life*—spending it with people you like and care about, doing work that you find meaningful, and giving yourself something to look forward to.

None of us knows why any of us are here. Life is a huge mystery. It's bigger than anything any one person can imagine. Just about the only thing I know for certain is that life is meant to be lived.

It's meant to be enjoyed, and I'm not talking about sitting on your couch with a beer while you watch television (not that there's anything wrong with that, once in a while). My advice is to get out of the house, go to new places, meet new people, and try new things. Don't listen to your fear—give in to your curiosity! Follow the part of your soul that wants to feel and have adventures. In the end, your life is nothing more than the sum of your experiences, the memories that you've made, so open yourself up to as many great moments as possible.

This is one reason why I have so many tattoos: I love them. Sure, they hurt a bit while they're being made, but I love being a canvas for art. Each tattoo on my body means something to me. By the time I got blown up, I had eight tattoos. After I was blown up, I had roughly six and a half. Now I have nine. Something tells me there will be more of these in my future.

I feel the same way about my piercings. I've had lots of them—in my ears, my tongue, my nipples. The pain is a rush, and it's fun to see how people react to them. People tell me that when I'm ninety years old and my body goes to shit, I'll be sorry. Maybe, maybe not. But I'll never get tired of telling the stories about how I got my tats. Everything that happens in my life, no matter how painful, becomes part of my story, and I regret not a single moment.

This might seem like an oddly sunny outlook for someone who has been blown up in combat, but I had to go through a very dark place in my life to find it. Roughly four months into my rehab at Walter Reed, I hit an emotional wall and sank into a major depression. It built up slowly and snuck up on me. Then, one day, it hit me full force at a moment when I was at my most vulnerable: in the shower.

Sitting there, naked under the spray and trying to wash myself, I knew it was impossible to pretend I didn't see what had happened to my body. There were no clothes to hide the uneven stumps of my legs or the mangled end of my left arm. All my scars were bare and plain to see. I tried not to let it get to me, but I couldn't stop the ugly thoughts that started filling my head: *Oh my God, I'm half a person. Jesus. Half a person. Oh my God.*

I lost it and started crying, right there, alone in the shower. My defenses fell apart. Every positive message I'd been telling myself felt like a lie. It was like being so far down a black hole that I was certain there was no way back up. I felt empty. Broken. It was a total meltdown. No one wants to end up there. And I'd been making so much progress that suddenly going backward like this was that much more of a hit, like running into a wall you thought you'd already climbed over. Now all that progress seemed like nothing compared to the road ahead of me.

Then it got worse. I began a downward spiral. Over the next two weeks, I suffered from panic attacks and chronic anxiety. My life was a living hell. I couldn't sleep, and I didn't want to talk to anybody. I didn't want to be alone, but I didn't want anybody around either. To be honest, I had no idea what I wanted. All I knew was that I was fucked. I felt as if every nerve and emotion in my body was pulling me in a different direction. I wanted to run away, but I didn't want to move. I didn't want to die, but I felt as if I didn't want to go on living. I was lost.

After two weeks of that unrelenting shit, I reached a breaking point and decided, *Damn it, I cannot* live *like this. I need to find a way out of this hole. There* has *to be way.* I simply refused to accept it. I felt like I had hit bottom, but even at the bottom of that hole,

I thought that there had to be some light at the top if I could only get to it somehow. I needed to do something. I mean, a pilot in a nosedive doesn't just sit there watching the ground rush up at him. He pulls back on the stick as hard as he can.

I finally figured out if I had no idea what to do, maybe someone else did. I'd been doing that thing I do—working so hard to be independent—that it took me two weeks of hell before I thought of asking for help. It's hard to do, but when you're in a place like this, no matter how much you don't want to admit it, just call someone. It might be embarrassing, you might feel vulnerable, but that's what friends are for, right? Your friends want to help. Give them that chance.

So I told a few old friends from home about some of what I was going through. One of them suggested I start listening to some music that would fuel my will to get up and fight for myself. "Y'know," one of them wrote in an e-mail, "Timmy's band is getting really big now. You should check them out." That was how I learned about Rise Against, a band featuring Tim McIlrath, a guy I'd known in high school. I bought a few of their CDs, and from the first moment I heard one, I was hooked. It was raw courage with power chords—exactly what I had needed, what I had been craving. Then I heard these lyrics from their song "Survive":

Life for you has been less than kind
So take a number, stand in line
We've all been sorry, we've all been hurt
But how we survive is what makes us who we are

Those lines stuck in my head from the first time I heard them, and I knew there was something important in them, something true. I made them the cornerstone of my recovery. That was the 180-degree attitude adjustment my soul had needed. It was like getting a wake-up call from my subconscious: "Stop whining, damn it! Get off your ass and live!" It felt as if I had grabbed the first rung of the ladder I needed to climb to get back to my life.

The next thing I did was tell my mom, "I need to get the hell out of here. I need to see real life again. I need to know what it is I'm trying to get well for." That was when she took me on the long weekend trip to Las Vegas that I told you about. Those three days were about one simple thing: having fun. It wasn't about therapy; it was just me, living my life and having a good time. That was what I had been missing. It made me feel human again.

After I came home from Las Vegas, I continued listening to Rise Against. I was rockin' to one of their CDs while I sat in front of the reflecting pond by the Malone House. Watching the ripples in the water, I thought about my life. *Y'know,* I told myself, *you just had three days of fun. While you were in Vegas, you didn't think about what had happened. It didn't matter that you'd lost your legs. No one treated you like a freak. You had a good time. So if you felt better while having a good time, then why not try to have a good time all the time? Don't put yourself in situations where you can feel sorry for yourself and get depressed. Get off your ass, go do new things, and have some fun. No one else can do this for you. It's all on you. Make yourself happy!*

I felt as if my eyes were open for the first time: if I wanted to be happy, it was up to me. That's the bottom line of it. You want to be in control of your own life, right? So who else has the power to make you happy? No matter what bad shit has happened to you, how you react to it and move forward is all on your shoulders. Sure, I couldn't change the fact that I lost both of my legs and an arm. And without a doubt there was going to be some pain and a whole lot of work to get myself mobile and independent again. I couldn't change the facts. But I did—and do—have the power over how I live my life.

Maybe some nasty shit has happened to you—an accident, illness, you lose someone you love, or whatever. It sucks and you can't change any of it. You've got no power over the past, only the future. You'll make yourself crazy if you obsess about what you could've or should've done, and it's a waste of time feeling angry about it or sorry for yourself. So screw that. The only thing you can do is decide to move forward and find happiness again.

Once I got that idea into my head, my whole point of view changed. I went out and just started having fun. Anything I felt like doing, any experience I wanted to have, I went out and tried it. I wanted to go to the mall by myself, so I went. I found the steepest hill and I tried to climb it. It didn't matter to me what anyone else said. No one—not my mom, my friends, or my doctors—could talk me out of things anymore. I understand that they were concerned for me and didn't want me to hurt myself, but obviously they wouldn't have had quite the same reaction if I still had all my limbs, and I refused to be defined by the injuries I had suffered. I'm more than that. I'm still a man, and I will not let anyone tell me that there's something I can't do. Maybe I can't do things the way other people do them, but if there's something I have my heart set on, I will always find a way to make it happen.

A lot of the things I do for fun these days—wakeboarding, skiing, waterskiing, and driving ATVs—I learned to do after I left rehab. I had to relearn how to skateboard. If I can push myself and do these things, anyone can. All it takes is the desire to get off your ass and really *live*. No matter what your condition, you can make the same choice. You want to go back to school? Do it. Learn a new skill, a new language? Why not? You can decide to do anything. You can decide to change your life. I know that's not going to happen right away for everyone. In a lot of cases, it's gonna take time. You need to be open to change, and you need to make an effort. Nobody will do it for you. No one will make you better. You need to be the one to change your own life.

Fun can be a huge tool to make yourself feel better. Find something—anything—that you like to do. Whether you make time for it only once a week, twice a week, or once a month, give yourself that release. Give yourself something to look forward to. It doesn't have to be stuff that some people think are crazy, like all my skiing and boarding. Read a book, watch a movie, play a board game with friends, whatever. It's easy to get into a routine of taking care of all your responsibilities, all the chores we all have to do to get by. Break it up with some fun.

Most important, never give in to self-pity. Don't waste time or energy feeling bad about things that have happened to you and that you can't change. More than once, people have asked me, "If you could travel back in time, would you change what happened to you on the day you were blown up in Iraq?" Most of them are shocked when I say, "No."

I've said it before, and I'll say it again: what happened to me that day was not a tragedy. I don't see it that way, and that's what matters. For me, that was just another event in my life, like getting married, or getting my first tattoo, or going to my first baseball game. That experience is part of what made me the person I am, and I *like* who I am. I don't want to change my past. I'd like to be whole-bodied again, but not if it means erasing my life and giving up who I am.

Thanks to the doors that were opened by my status as a wounded veteran, I've been to some amazing places, met wonderful people, and done a number of really cool things.

Since coming home from Iraq, I've been on the cover of *Esquire* magazine, thrown out the first pitch at a Chicago Cubs game, driven in a NASCAR race, gone white-water rafting in the Grand Canyon, met James Gandolfini and Gary Sinise, and acted on television and in an Oscar-nominated feature film. I've lived my life on my own terms. How many people ever get to say that? How many people get the chance to live the way that I have?

I regret nothing. I love my life.

Now I need to get heavy on you for a second. A big part of making this idea of mine work in real life is being responsible about how we have fun. I believe that my fun shouldn't come at someone else's expense. My right to do what I want ends at the point where I start screwing up someone else's fun. This goes way beyond not bothering your neighbor by turning up your stereo too loud. What I'm talking about here is taking a second to think about how the things you do affect other people, not just next door but around the world.

I like driving ATVs, and as vehicles go, they're pretty fuel-efficient. But if it was possible for me to have just as much fun riding a quad without burning gasoline, I would do it. If there was an all-electric ATV that performed as well as the one I have now, I would switch in a heartbeat. Why? Because it would make less pollution and conserve gasoline for some other more important job (like farming, for instance). This isn't about being a tree hugger or some kind of environmental wacko. If I can have my fun without making messes for other people to clean up, I think that's better. As the Boy Scouts of America say, "Leave each place better than you found it." I think that's a lesson we should all try to follow.

No one would ever call me a bleeding heart, but I think it's good to feel and show compassion for other people. I'm talking beyond family and friends. That's important, sure, but just being good to the people closest to you won't always help the big picture. Think about how much energy, fuel, food, and water are consumed each day by the industrialized countries of the world. Now take a second to remember that there are millions of people, mostly kids, dying each day in places like sub-Saharan Africa, Southeast Asia, and rural India because they don't have enough food, clean water, or medicine. Does that seem right to you? I think it's kind of fucked up. It's like we're having a big, fat picnic while surrounded by a crowd of starving people who are dying and being forced to watch us eat.

Most of us tune out those stories on the news, and we don't think about them while we're chowing down at our backyard barbecues— but maybe we should. Remember what I said about being responsible in how you have fun? This is part of what I'm talking about. I want to live in a world in which everyone everywhere can enjoy their lives to the fullest. To make that happen, we'd have to get serious about changing our priorities, not just as a nation but as a species. Human beings would have to stop fighting over bullshit and get on the same page.

I know, it's a crazy idea, but if enough of us get behind it, it can work. We each need to start by improving our own lives, and then we need to work on improving the lives of the people closest to us—our friends and families. Next, instead of just complaining about the problems in your neighborhood, town, or city, start pitching in and creating solutions. Become a force for positive change. Make other people's lives better, not just your own. The more good that you do, the more people who will want to join you and be part of what you're doing. It's the snowball effect on a grand scale: the only way to change the world is to start small, one life at a time, and keep pushing forward until the momentum for change becomes unstoppable.

We can build a better world for everyone. All it takes is the willingness to do the work.

This isn't the kind of change that can happen overnight, but if we all started giving a damn about one another, I think we could make a real difference in less time than you'd think. I also think that regardless of our spiritual or religious beliefs, we have a moral duty to try. If you think there is more to our existence than just our time on earth—in other words, if you believe in an afterlife or in reincarnation—then you should make an effort to keep this planet clean and be good to all the people in it because someday you might have to answer for the life you've lived and the choices you've made. On the other hand, if you believe that this life is all there is, and that there is no life after death, then it's even *more* important that you be considerate about how you use this world's resources and treat your fellow human beings. If this one trip through life is all that any of us will ever know, and there is no "great reward" after death for those who have suffered in life, then we owe it to one another to make this the best time we can for all of us around the world, and for everyone who's going to come along after we're gone.

No matter what you believe in, my point is this: we all have to make our journeys together, so let's make them awesome and fun. I think that maybe *Bill & Ted's Excellent Adventure* said it best: "Be excellent to each other—and party on, dudes!"

ACKNOWLEDGMENTS

I want to offer my many thanks to the following people without whom this book would never have happened.

Dick McLane, who took a punk military kid and opened his eyes to a world of new possibilities and who always has my back.

Deidre Knight and David Mack for using their collective talents; without their help and support this book would never have been completed.

Scott Meuser for giving me opportunity and support and having the faith in me to get the job done.

All the cool people I've met in Pennsylvania for their support and friendship.

Paul Jenkins for encouraging me to write this book and convincing me it was possible.

The staff at Walter Reed for giving me the support and tools for getting my life back. And a special shout-out to nurse "Special K" in the ICU unit of Walter Reed.

My close friend Sunshine, who was my roommate when I first returned from Walter Reed, for his support, companionship, understanding, and being there through "thick and thin."

231

ACKNOWLEDGMENTS

Timmy McIlrath and Rise Against for their musical talents and creativity, which allowed me to make that first, important step in getting my life back.

Michael Wait for putting the damn tourniquets on right and saving my life. Michael, thank you.

ABOUT THE AUTHOR

Bryan Anderson resides in the Chicago area nearby his parents, Jim and Janet, identical twin brother, Bob, and younger sister, Briana. In addition to academic excellence, Bryan excelled in sports during his high school years and competed as an accomplished gymnast in state-level competitions. Following graduation, he worked for American Airlines as a ground-crew chief at O'Hare Airport.

Bryan enlisted in the Army in April 2001 and had a "ship out" date of September 11, 2001. He served two tours of duty in Iraq and was stationed in the Baghdad area. He attained the rank of sergeant in the military police, conducted police training courses in Iraq, and gained additional law enforcement experience at Leavenworth Federal Penitentiary as a prison guard.

In October 2005, Bryan was injured by an improvised explosive device (IED) that resulted in the loss of both his legs and his left hand. As a result of his injuries, he was awarded a Purple Heart. Bryan received rehabilitation for a period of thirteen months at Walter Reed Army Hospital. He is one of the few triple amputees to have survived his injuries in Iraq.

Bryan's story has received extensive media coverage, including two feature articles in *Esquire* magazine (one a cover shot in January 2007) as well as numerous articles in major newspapers and publications, from his hometown paper, the *Chicago Sun-Times*, to the *Los Angeles Times* and the *New York Times*.

Bryan has appeared in the HBO documentary *Alive Day Memories: Home from Iraq* and in a *CSI: NY* episode titled "DOA for a Day." He also appears in the 2008 Golden Globe Award–winning film *The Wrestler*, starring Mickey Rourke and Marisa Tomei. In addition, Bryan was interviewed by MTV News's *Choose or Lose* "Street Team" and has appeared on the daytime drama *All My Children*.

Bryan is the national spokesman for Quantum Rehab, a division of Pride Mobility Corp., and travels the country making numerous personal appearances in major rehab facilities while delivering his message of perseverance and determination. In addition, he is a spokesman for USA Cares, a nonprofit organization based in Radcliff, Kentucky, that is focused on assisting post-9/11 veterans in times of need.

Bryan is an energetic and enthusiastic individual who enjoys challenging his limits. He snowboards, wakeboards, white-water rafts, and rock climbs. He loves to travel and enjoys meeting new people.

His official website is www.andersonactive.com/.

ABOUT THE COAUTHOR

David Mack is the national best-selling author of nearly twenty novels, including *Wildfire, Harbinger, Reap the Whirlwind, Precipice, Road of Bones, Promises Broken,* and the *Star Trek Destiny* trilogy: *Gods of Night, Mere Mortals,* and *Lost Souls.* He developed the *Star Trek Vanguard* series concept with editor Marco Palmieri. His first work of original fiction is the critically acclaimed supernatural thriller *The Calling.*

In addition to novels, Mack's writing credits span several media, including television (for episodes of *Star Trek: Deep Space Nine*), film, short fiction, magazines, newspapers, comic books, computer games, radio, and the Internet.

His upcoming novels include the *Star Trek: Mirror Universe* adventure *Rise Like Lions* and a new original supernatural thriller.

Visit his official website, http://www.davidmack.pro, and follow him on Twitter @DavidAlanMack.